NECESSARY SKILLS
FOR THE WORKFORCE

Job Readiness

By Vivian Bernstein

CONSULTANTS

Dee Marie Boydstun
Literacy Coordinator
Black Hawk College
Moline, Illinois

Marie S. Olsen
Learning Center Coordinator
for Rio Salado Community College
at Maricopa Skill Center
Phoenix, Arizona

John C. Ritter
Teacher, Education Programs
Oregon Women's Correctional Center
Salem, Oregon

STECK-VAUGHN
COMPANY
ELEMENTARY • SECONDARY • ADULT • LIBRARY

ABOUT THE AUTHOR

Vivian Bernstein is the author of *America's Story, World History and You, World Geography and You, American Government,* and *Decisions for Health.* She received her Master of Arts degree from New York University. Bernstein is active with professional organizations in social studies, education, and reading. She gives presentations to school faculties and professional groups about content area reading. Bernstein was a teacher in the New York City Public School System for a number of years.

CREDITS

Cover Photography: (crossing street) © Stock Boston, (job board) © Aneal Vohra/Unicorn Stock Photos, (interview) © Steven Lunetta/ PhotoEdit

All photos by Park Street with the following exceptions.
p. 5 © Aneal Vohra/Unicorn Photos; p. 6 © Rhoda Sidney/ PhotoEdit; p.7 © Rich Baker/Unicorn Photos; p. 9 © Myrleen Ferguson/ PhotoEdit; p. 15 David Omer; p. 16 © Michael Grecco/ Stock Boston; pp. 17, 18, 19 David Omer; pp. 42, 43 Reagan Bradshaw; p. 51 Rick Williams; p. 52 © Tony Freeman/PhotoEdit; p. 53 © Stephen Frasch/ Stock Boston; p. 54 © Michael Dwyer/ Stock Boston; p. 60 Billy E. Barnes/Stock Boston; p. 61 © Arni Katz/Unicorn Photos; p. 65 © Bob Daemmrich/Stock Boston; p. 78 © David M. Grossman/Photo Researchers; p. 99 © Erika Stone/ Photo Researchers; p. 100 © Ellis Herwig/Stock Boston; p. 107 © Ellis Herwig/Stock Boston; p. 109 © Gale Zucker/Stock Boston; p. 110 © Bob Daemmrich/Stock Boston.

We would like to express our appreciation to all local, state, and national governmental agencies that helped in the preparation of this book. In particular, we would like to thank the following for providing information and forms for the workshops:

   Social Security Administration
   Equal Employment Opportunity Commission

Portion of *Safety Manual for an Electric Utility* reproduced with permission of the American Public Power Association. To obtain an American Public Power Association safety manual, write or call APPA, 2301 M Street, NW, Washington, DC 20037. (202) 467-2953.

ISBN 0–8172–6381–0

Printed in the United States of America.   **1 2 3 4 5 6 7 8 9 0 RP 01 00 99 98 97 96**

CONTENTS

Necessary Skills for the Workforce: Job Readiness can help you learn skills to be successful in the workplace and will show you how to use these skills. Each chapter in this book includes a lesson followed by a workshop and exercises. One workshop in this book is "Completing a Job Application." What kind of applications have you filled out?

_____

_____

_____

In the "Thinking and Writing" exercise, you will be asked to write in your journal. Your journal can be a notebook or just a group of pages. Writing in a journal helps you gather your thoughts and put them on paper. One exercise in this book asks you to think about the kind of job you want and then write a letter of application to a possible employer. Thinking and writing about problems can help you find answers. Try it here. Think about questions or problems you may have about getting a job or about work. On the lines below, tell how you think this book will help you.

_____

_____

_____

There are an index, a glossary, and an answer key in the back of this book. These features can help you use this book independently.

Have fun working through this book. Then enjoy your new skills!

CHAPTER 1

Choosing the Right Kind of Work

- What are five reasons for getting a job?
- How do you know if a job is right for you?
- How can you improve yourself so you can get a better job?

There are thousands of different kinds of jobs. Some jobs are desk jobs. Other jobs allow you to work outdoors. Choosing the right kind of work is important. With the right job, you will enjoy working. As you read this chapter, you will learn how to find a job that is right for you.

Reasons for Getting a Job

There are five reasons for working. First, you will earn money. You will have money to buy what you need to live. You can save money to buy some of the things you really want.

Second, working makes you have self-respect. You will feel proud that you can earn money for doing a job. You will feel important when you see that you can do your job well.

Third, your life will be more interesting. You will have something to do and a place to go. You will be learning new skills at your job.

Fourth, you will meet new people. You may eat lunch with some of these people. They may become your friends. You may decide to get together after work.

Fifth, you will be a good **role model** for your children and other family members. Your children will see you going to work. They will want to be like you. When they are old enough, they will want to work, too.

A **role model** is a person who sets an example for others to follow.

Your job will help you earn money to buy what you want and need.

■

Try to find a job that is interesting to you.

Knowing What Job Is Right for You

You will enjoy working if you choose a job that is right for you. To find the right job, first understand yourself.

Think about your **talents.** Do you have a special talent for art? Are you good at fixing things or putting things together? Perhaps you have a talent for getting along well with all kinds of people. Your talent might be caring for young children. You want to find a job that allows you to use your talents.

Think about your **personality.** Do you enjoy being part of a large crowd? Are you happier being with just one good friend? Do you enjoy talking? Would you rather listen to other people talk? Understanding your personality will help you decide on the kind of job that is right for you.

Think about your interests. Are you interested in woodworking? Are you interested in caring for plants or animals? Perhaps you have an interest in using different kinds of tools and machines. You want a job where you can do work that interests you. You want a job that you enjoy.

Your **talents** are your special skills.

Your **personality** is the special way you act and feel.

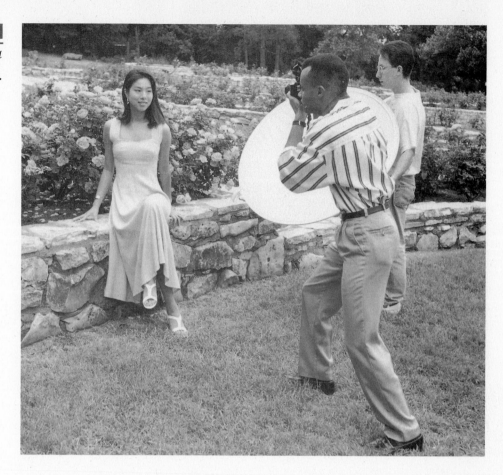

Your **values** are the ideas, beliefs, and actions that are important to you.

Think about your **values.** Your values are actions and ideas that are important to you. For some people being kind and helping others are important values. Enjoying time with friends and exercising may be some of your values. Your job can help you keep your values. Perhaps spending time with your family on weekends is one of your values. Then you will not want to work on Saturdays and Sundays.

Finding the Right Job Area

There are many different kinds of jobs. How do you choose the kind of job that is right for you? You start by thinking about the things you enjoy doing. Then think about your interests and personality. Think about your talents and values. Study the job areas chart on pages 10 and 11. Use the chart to learn about many kinds of jobs. Then choose a job area that fits your interests, talents, values, and personality.

Evan Jones used this chart to choose a job. Evan loves art. So he wanted to work in the job area called "Art." He thought about his interests and personality. He enjoys working with his hands. He has a quiet personality. He likes working alone and having his own business. So he decided to become a sign painter. Evan is a lucky person. He can earn money doing what he enjoys and what he does well.

You can get a better job by improving your skills. Having a high school diploma or a GED diploma will help you get a better job. You may also do **volunteer** work. Volunteer work gives you job experience. Some jobs may offer to train you. Be willing to learn new skills.

Working at the right job will help you enjoy life. You will earn money and feel proud of yourself. Know your interests and values. Understand your talents and personality. Then you can choose a job that is right for you.

When you **volunteer,** you do a job without getting paid.

Volunteer work can give you job experience. It may lead to full-time work.

Job Area	Types of Jobs	Skills for the Job
Sales	▪ car salesperson ▪ store salesperson ▪ insurance agent ▪ travel agent	▪ You may need a high school education. ▪ Are you friendly? ▪ Do you enjoy talking to other people? ▪ Are you a good listener?
Industrial Work	▪ machine operator ▪ packager ▪ inspector ▪ butcher	▪ You may be able to learn skills on the job. ▪ Do you enjoy using machines? ▪ Can you follow instructions? ▪ Do you enjoy doing the same job over and over again?
Art	▪ photographer ▪ floral designer ▪ musician ▪ jewelry maker ▪ sign painter	▪ You may need special training. ▪ Do you know how to play an instrument well? ▪ Do you know how to draw or paint? ▪ Do you know how to use a camera? ▪ Do you like to make things?
Science	▪ lab technician ▪ lab assistant	▪ You may need special courses after high school. ▪ Do you like math and science? ▪ Do you follow directions well?
Education	▪ teacher's aide ▪ teacher ▪ library aide ▪ librarian	▪ You must finish high school. Most jobs require college. ▪ Do you like to help others learn?
Office Work	▪ telephone operator ▪ file clerk ▪ typist ▪ word processor ▪ receptionist ▪ secretary	▪ Do you like to talk on the telephone? ▪ Do you know how to keep records? ▪ Do you know how to file? ▪ Do you like to work indoors at a desk? ▪ Do you like typing and word processing? ▪ Do you like computer work?
Animal Care	▪ pet store worker ▪ veterinarian's aide ▪ animal trainer ▪ groomer	▪ Do you like being with animals? ▪ Do you like physical work?
Service	▪ police officer ▪ firefighter ▪ letter carrier ▪ garbage collector ▪ cook ▪ waiter ▪ cashier ▪ maintenance worker ▪ house cleaner	▪ You must finish high school for many jobs. ▪ Do you enjoy helping others? ▪ Are you healthy and strong?

Job Area	Types of Jobs	Skills for the Job
Mechanical Work	■ car mechanic ■ equipment repairer	■ You must take courses or work as an **apprentice**, learning skills on the job. ■ Do you like to work with tools? ■ Do you like to fix things? ■ Can you do math?
Construction	■ electrician ■ carpenter ■ bricklayer ■ painter ■ plumber ■ roofer	■ You may need courses. You can work as an apprentice, learning skills on the job. ■ Do you like to work with tools? ■ Do you enjoy outdoor work?
Transportation	■ bus driver ■ taxi driver ■ truck driver ■ flight attendant	■ You may need to take a special course and pass a test. ■ Do you like to meet new people? ■ Do you like to travel?
Health Care	■ nursing aide ■ dental assistant ■ ambulance attendant ■ home care aide ■ orderly ■ physical therapist	■ You may need special courses. ■ Do you like helping people who are old or sick? ■ Are you strong enough to lift an adult?
Child Care	■ day-care worker ■ preschool aide ■ preschool teacher	■ You may have to have a license. ■ Do you like children? ■ Are you calm when someone is hurt or sick?
Beauty Services	■ barber ■ manicurist ■ hairdresser	■ You must pass a course and get a license. ■ Do you like working with your hands? ■ Do you enjoy helping people?

List other job areas and jobs that interest you. Think about the skills these jobs require.

Finding Out About Yourself

Read each sentence below. Think about how you feel about each idea. Then show how you feel by writing a number next to the sentence. Use the numbers this way:

1 = very much   2 = a little   3 = not at all

After you finish, read all the sentences you marked with the number 1 or 2. Then look at the job areas chart on pages 10 and 11. Choose one job area that would help you use your skills, interests, and values. You can also learn about other kinds of jobs and job areas at your library.

_____ 1. I enjoy meeting and talking to people.

_____ 2. I enjoy traveling.

_____ 3. I enjoy doing the same job again and again.

_____ 4. I want to help other people as much as I can.

_____ 5. I want a job where I can use my math skills.

_____ 6. I enjoy doing art work.

_____ 7. I enjoy working with my hands.

_____ 8. I enjoy helping others learn.

_____ 9. I enjoy fixing things.

_____ 10. I enjoy working with tools and machines.

_____ 11. I enjoy doing typing and word processing.

_____ 12. I enjoy computer work.

_____ 13. I enjoy caring for animals.

_____ 14. I enjoy caring for children.

_____ 15. I enjoy office work.

_____ 16. I like to work outdoors.

_____ 17. I like to use my physical strength when I work.

_____ 18. I enjoy science.

CHECK YOUR SKILLS

WORKSHOP PRACTICE: Finding the Right Kind of Work

Look back at the job areas chart on pages 10 and 11 to answer the following questions.

1. What skills do you need to work at a pet store?

   _____

   _____

2. Name four kinds of jobs in the area of construction work.

   _____

   _____

3. What skills do you need for sales work?

   _____

   _____

4. Name four kinds of health care jobs.

   _____

   _____

5. What skills do you need for office work?

   _____

   _____

6. Name four kinds of service jobs.

   _____

   _____

COMPREHENSION: True or False

Write True next to each sentence that is true. Write False next to each sentence that is false. There are two false sentences.

_____ 1. Going to work helps you feel proud and important.

_____ 2. You will enjoy a job where you can use your talents.

_____ 3. Your personality is not important when you choose a job.

_____ 4. A job can help you keep your values.

_____ 5. Improving your skills will not help you get a better job.

On the lines that follow, rewrite the false sentences to make them true.

_____

_____

_____

_____

VOCABULARY: Matching

Match the vocabulary word in Group B with a definition in Group A. Write the letter of the answer on the line.

Group A

_____ 1. This is a person who sets a good example for others to follow.

_____ 2. This is someone who learns skills on the job.

_____ 3. This is the special way you act and feel.

_____ 4. Your special skills are called this.

_____ 5. These are the ideas and beliefs that are important to you.

Group B

a. apprentice

b. talents

c. values

d. role model

e. personality

Thinking and Writing

Study the job areas chart on pages 10 and 11. Choose one job area that you think would be right for you. In your journal, explain which jobs you want to do and why those jobs may be right for you.

CHAPTER 2

FINDING A JOB

THINK ABOUT AS YOU READ

■ How can your friends help you get a job?

■ How are state employment agencies different from private ones?

■ How can you use the newspaper to find job information?

Linda Gonzalez worked for a company that moved to a different state. Linda needs to find a new job. She wants to start finding job information about different jobs.

In this chapter you will learn how to find job information. You can use this information to find the right kind of job.

■

You can find job information many different places. The newspaper is one source.

How to Start Looking for a Job

Tell everyone you know that you are looking for work. This is the best way to find a job. Tell your family and friends. Talk to them about the kind of job you want. You may get job leads or job information from them. They can ask their **employer** if there are any job openings where they work.

You will want lots of people to know that you are looking for a job. As more people learn that you need work, they will tell others. Some of their employers may want you to **apply** for a job.

There are bulletin boards in schools, supermarkets, and community centers. Some employers write down job information on small cards. Then they put the job information cards on these bulletin boards.

You may see a job that interests you on a bulletin board. Call the employer at once. Employers often find workers for these jobs quickly.

An **employer** is a person or business that people work for.

To **apply** for a job means to ask for a job and then prepare forms or letters to get the job.

Job bulletin boards can give you job leads.

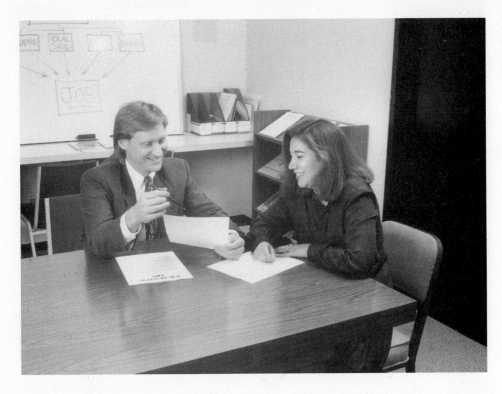

Employment Agencies

You may get the job you want through an **employment agency.** There are two kinds of agencies. They are private agencies and state agencies. Private agencies charge **fees.** Sometimes the fee is paid by the employer. Sometimes it must be paid by the worker. State employment offices are run by state governments. Every state has an employment agency. State agencies do not charge fees.

You can find private employment agencies listed in the Yellow Pages of the telephone book. Private agencies are also listed in the **classified ads** of the newspaper.

You may want a private agency to help you find a job. Call one of these agencies. You will be asked to visit the agency. You will meet with a **job counselor** there. The counselor will test your skills to find out what kind of work you can do. The agency will send you for **job interviews** at jobs that match your skills.

An **employment agency** is a group of people who work to find jobs for others.

Fees are the money people pay when they receive services.

Classified ads are ads in the newspaper for jobs, houses, and apartments.

A **job counselor** is a person at an employment agency who helps you find a job.

A **job interview** is a meeting between an employer and a person who wants a job.

17

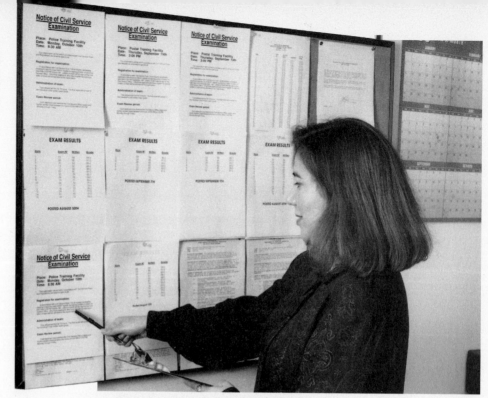

An **application** is the form you fill out to apply for a job.

You can try to get a job through your state employment agency. Go to an agency office near your home. You will fill out a job **application.** Then you will meet with a job counselor.

Perhaps you are unsure of the kind of job you want. The counselor can give you a special test to find out about your talents and skills. You may also take an interest test to find out what kind of work you would enjoy doing. It takes a few weeks for the counselor to get the results from your test. Then the counselor will help you choose the best kind of job for you. You will be sent for interviews. These interviews can lead to good jobs.

State agencies are often very busy. It is best to go to your state agency early in the morning.

Civil Service Jobs

Civil service jobs are jobs with the government.

Millions of people enjoy working for the government. They have **civil service jobs.** They may work for the United States government. For example, working for the post office is a civil service job. These jobs pay good salaries and good benefits. You have to take a test to get a civil service job.

To take the civil service test, find out when it will be given. Look up the telephone numbers of the United States government in the White Pages. Some phone books have government telephone numbers in the Blue Pages. Then look for the heading "Postal Service." Under Postal Service, look for a listing about employment information. Call that number and ask about how to sign up for the civil service test. Follow those directions. When you take the test, you will also find out about other civil service jobs.

Newspaper Ads and Personnel Offices

Newspapers have classified ads. Many of these ads are for jobs. They are grouped together under "Help Wanted" headings. Job ads are listed in alphabetical order. Check the Help Wanted pages every day. Each day there will be new ads in the newspaper.

Employers often find workers quickly for jobs that are in the newspaper. If you see a job ad that interests you, call about that job right away.

Apply at the personnel office of large companies.

Help Wanted ads provide information about jobs. They may tell where the job is and what skills you need for the job. They tell you how you can apply for the job.

It takes practice to read and understand Help Wanted ads. The chart on page 22 lists abbreviations that are found in many ads. The ad below is for a deli cook. From the ad you can learn that the deli cook will earn $275 a week. You also learn that it is a full-time job. The ad tells you that the employer would like to give this job to a person with **experience.**

Experience is the past practice and training you have from doing a job before.

Deli Cook
F/T $275 wk. Busy downtown deli. Exp. pref., non-smoker. Call for information 866-2543

Personnel are the people who work for a business or employer.

Some large companies have their own **personnel** offices. You can go to one of these personnel offices and ask about getting a job. Fill out an application for a job. You may be called for a job interview when there is a job opening.

There are many ways to get information about job openings. Your family and friends may have information. You will want to check bulletin boards and Help Wanted ads. An employment agency may help you find a job. Getting information about job openings will help you find a job that is right for you.

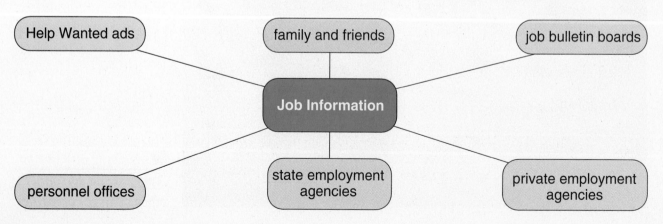

Reading the Help Wanted Ads

Learning to read the Help Wanted ads may help you find a job. On this page are some Help Wanted ads from a newspaper. They are in alphabetical order. Many ads use abbreviations to save space. Use the abbreviations chart on page 22 to understand the ads.

Help Wanted	Help Wanted	Help Wanted
AUTO MECH Needed Installation of a/c & other parts. Exp. pref. Will train. Top pay w/exp. Central Car Repairs. Call 889-1000	⇨ **DELIVERY—GENERAL** ⇦ **START NOW $250/WEEK** Many pos. avail. Learn all aspects of import/export bus. No exp. nec. Car req. Call Lynn 343-5678	NURSE'S AIDES P/T positions avail. Nursing home on 82nd Ave. Must be certified. Call Mrs. Smith 728-9007
CONSTRUCTION Jobs for home improvement co., 5 yrs. exp. req. Must be organized. Meet demands and deadlines of industry. Resume only to: Ace Home Improvement PO Box 146 Portland, OR 97216	**FACTORY HELP F/T** for packaging company. Days 8:30–5:15 $5 per hr. Nights 5:30 pm–2 am $5.50 per hr. Apply in person. Call Carl Wilson, 221-6660	**WAITER/WAITRESS** We offer year-round work P/T, F/T with flexible hrs. & competitive wages. Includes training program. Call Crystal Country Club between 1 pm & 5 pm 269-6000
COOK PIZZA, PASTA Exp'd. Must be fast. Very busy pizza shop. Good opportunity! 402-2000 after 10 am	MAINTENANCE Eve. maint. person, light painting, cleaning, answering phones, taking msg. Ben. Washington County. Call 9–2 M–F 678-5623	WAREHOUSE DISTRIBUTION START NOW! $280/WK. World Import Co. has 20 F/T pos. avail. Learn all aspects. No exp. nec. Call Ana 233-3700

■ ■ ■

Use the ads and the abbreviations chart to answer the following questions.

1. Leroy Smith is looking for a factory job. Find the ad he would be interested in.

   a. What kind of company needs factory help? _____

   b. What is the pay for the day shift? _____

2. Kathy Rivas is looking for a job at a nursing home. Find the ad she will read.

   a. Is this job full-time or part-time? _____

   b. What phone number should Kathy call? _____

3. Bob Johnson is looking for a construction job. Find the ad for this type of work.

   a. What type of construction work is it? _____

   b. How much experience is required? _____

Abbreviations Used in Help Wanted Ads

a/c	air conditioning	**lic.**	license
am	morning	**mach.**	machine
appt.	appointment	**maint.**	maintenance
asst.	assistant (helper)	**manuf.**	manufacturing
avail.	available	**mech.**	mechanic, mechanical
ben.	benefits	**M–F**	Monday through Friday
bus.	business	**mo.**	month
cert.	certified, certificate	**msg.**	message
co.	company	**nec.**	necessary
const.	construction	**ofc.**	office
dept.	department	**pd.**	paid
elec.	electric	**pm**	afternoon or evening
EOE	Equal Opportunity Employer	**pos.**	position
etc.	and so on	**pref.**	preferred
eve.	evening	**P/T**	part-time
exp.	experience	**ref.**	references
exp'd.	experienced	**req.**	required
F/T	full-time	**sal.**	salary
gd.	good	**sec.**	secretary
grad.	graduate	**temp.**	temporary
hosp.	hospital	**typ.**	typing
hr.	hour	**w/**	with
immed.	immediate	**wk.**	week
incl.	including	**WP**	word processing
info.	information	**yr.**	year

WORKSHOP PRACTICE: Using Abbreviations

Understanding ad abbreviations will help you read Help Wanted ads. Write the meaning next to each abbreviation on this page. Use the chart on page 22 to help you.

1. ben. _____

2. eve. _____

3. F/T _____

4. req. _____

5. M–F _____

6. wk. _____

7. exp. pref. _____

8. hr. _____

9. am _____

10. pm _____

11. mech. _____

12. nec. _____

COMPREHENSION: Write the Answer

Write one or more sentences to answer each question.

1. Why should you tell your family and friends you are looking for work?

   _____

   _____

2. How can your state employment agency help you get a job?

   _____

   _____

3. How is a private employment agency different from a state agency?

   _____

   _____

4. What do you have to do to get a civil service job?

_____

_____

5. What are four ways to find out about job openings?

_____

_____

VOCABULARY: Finish the Sentence

Choose one of the following words or phrases to complete each sentence. Write the word or phrase on the correct line.

employer
experience
fee
classified ads
personnel
application

1. The person you work for is your

   _____ .

2. The money paid to private employment agencies is

   their _____ .

3. The form you fill out to apply for a job is a job

   _____ .

4. Job openings are listed in the newspaper

   _____ .

5. The people who work for a business are called the

   _____ .

6. The practice and training you have had at work is your

   job _____ .

Thinking and Writing

Think about different ways you can get information about job openings. Explain in your journal which ways you would want to use to find a job.

CHAPTER 3

APPLYING FOR A JOB

THINK ABOUT AS YOU READ

- How do you apply for a job by phone?
- What kinds of letters do you write to apply for a job?
- When do you apply for a job in person?

José Martinez wants to get a job as a pet store worker. He has information about job openings. But he is not sure of the best way to apply for these jobs. José could call the places. Or he could write letters. He could go to the places in person. In this chapter you will learn about different ways you can apply for a job.

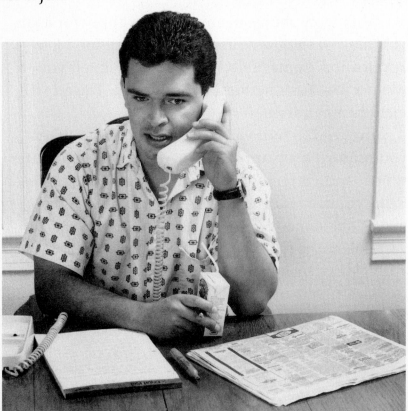

Your first job contact
may be by phone.

Applying for a Job by Phone

Sometimes the best way to apply for a job is by phone. You can apply by phone to answer a Help Wanted ad that has a phone number to call. Look back at the Help Wanted ads on page 21. You can see that most of these ads tell people to apply by phone. You can also apply by phone if your friend or relative gives you a job lead with a phone number.

You will want to make a good **impression** when you apply for a job by phone. Speak clearly and politely. Use correct English.

Plan what you want to say before you make your phone call. Tell the person who answers your call that you want to apply for a job. The person who answers the phone may send you a job application. Then you give your name and address. The person may ask you to come in to pick up a job application. Or you may need to write a letter asking for a job application. Ask for the employer's address. Be sure you know how and where to get a job application before you end your phone call.

Applying for a Job by Letter

When you phone an employer to apply for a job, you may be told to write a letter asking for a job application. Some Help Wanted ads will tell you to write a letter asking for an application. The ad will include an address.

You need to write a short business letter when you **request** a job application. Make sure your letter is neat and correctly written. Include your address. Read your letter carefully before you send it. You may want someone else to check it for you.

Look at the letter José wrote to request a job application. José wrote his letter very neatly. You can also type your letter to request a job application. Some libraries have typewriters and computers you can use for a small fee.

You make an **impression** when you affect the way another person thinks and feels about you.

To **request** means to ask for something.

26

22 Maple Street
Los Angeles, CA 90046
February 1, 1994

Ms. Ann Peters
Personnel Director
Pet Palace
605 Franklin Avenue
Los Angeles, CA 90046

Dear Ms. Peters:

    I saw your store's Help Wanted ad for a pet store worker. I have experience working in a pet store, and I would like to apply for the job.

    Please send me a job application.

Sincerely,

José Martinez

Other Help Wanted ads will say that you can apply for a job by writing a **letter of application.** A letter of application is sometimes used instead of a job application. This type of letter tells the employer a lot about you. You want to show the employer that you are the best person for the job.

Your letter of application includes the following information.

1. the kind of job you are applying for

2. your education

3. your work experience

4. your special skills that will help you do a good job

5. a request for an interview

6. a sentence that says you can provide the names of **references**

7. your phone number

Your letter of application is written like a business letter. Make sure your letter has no spelling mistakes. Do not cross out words. Look at the letter of application José wrote to apply for a job at Pets Unlimited. José's letter tells the employer that he has the experience, skills, and interest to do a good job.

Your letter of application will speak for you.

22 Maple Street
Los Angeles, CA 90046
February 1, 1994

Mr. Allen Mills
Pets Unlimited
175 W. 9th Street
Los Angeles, CA 90015

Dear Mr. Mills:

I learned from a Help Wanted ad in the <u>Los Angeles Times</u> that your store needs a person to care for animals.

I graduated from high school in June 1992. In high school I studied typing and business math.

From 1992 until the end of 1993, I was a pet store worker at Petland on Hillside Avenue. I also did this work during the summers of 1990 and 1991 at John's Pet World. I really enjoy caring for animals and helping customers. Since I am also a weight lifter, I am quite strong. I can handle large, heavy dogs easily.

I can provide the names of references upon request.

I would like to set up an interview. Please call me at 375-2865 after 4:00 p.m.

Sincerely,

José Martinez

José Martinez

Make a good first impression.

Applying for a Job in Person

Sometimes an employment agency will give you the address of an employer. The job counselor may tell you to go to the employer to apply in person. Sometimes Help Wanted ads will give you an address without a phone number. Then you have to apply for the job in person. Be sure to dress neatly when you apply for a job in person.

Job Applications and Resumes

For most jobs you will need to fill out a job application. Filling out the form neatly and correctly will help you get a job. Use a pen and spell correctly. Some employers allow people to fill out the application at home. If you do it at home, you can ask for help with some of the questions. Get an extra copy of the job application to practice on.

The Necessary Skills Workshop on pages 34–37 shows you how to complete a job application. Most applications ask almost the same questions. Fill out the application in the Workshop. You can use it as a guide when you have to fill out other applications. Take it with you when you apply for a job in person.

Be prepared to give the names of two or three people. These people are your references. Always ask these people if you may use them for references. A reference may be your past employer. It may be someone who has known you for a long time. Do not use family members for references.

Always tell the truth on your applications. The law says an employer cannot refuse to **hire** you because you have a **disability.** The employer cannot refuse to hire you because of your sex, race, age, or religion.

Sometimes an employer will ask for a **resume** when you apply for a job. Some employers use resumes instead of job applications to hire workers. Prepare a resume and have it ready. Then you can give it to an employer who asks for it.

A good resume can help you get a job. Include information about your work experience, education, and skills. You can put the information in any order. You want the employer to notice your strongest points first.

To **hire** means to give a person a job and pay them for their work.

A **disability** is a problem that makes a person less able to do certain things. If you have a hearing disability, then you do not hear very well.

A **resume** is a summary of information about your education and skills.

Have someone help you review your letters and resume.

Be prepared to give a resume if the employer asks for one.

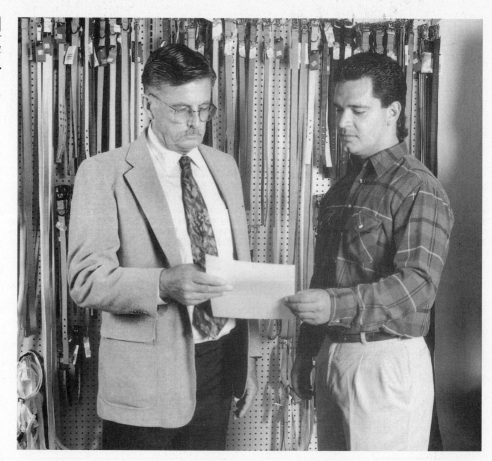

Look at the resume José prepared on page 33. José listed his skills first. His skills show that he would make a good pet store worker. José listed his work experience next. He has worked in a pet store before. This experience can help him get the job.

You may list two or three references on your resume. Or you can say that the names of references will be given if requested. Do not leave out this part.

Have your resume typed neatly on one sheet of paper. You want your resume to make a good impression for you.

You may fill out a job application when you apply for a job. You may need to make phone calls. You may need to write a letter or have a resume. Practice what you are going to say before you phone. Write a practice letter. Prepare a resume. Get someone to read them before you send them. Applying for a job correctly will help you get the job you want.

José F. Martinez

22 Maple Street • Los Angeles, CA 90046 • (213) 375-2865

Job Objective: Pet Store Worker

Skills

- experienced pet store worker
- friendly to customers
- patient with animals
- enjoy all kinds of pets
- strong (weight lifter)
- can type 45 words a minute

Employment Experience

1992-1993   Pet store worker
Petland
24 Hillside Avenue, Los Angeles, CA 90046

1990, 1991   Pet store worker
(Summers)   John's Pet World
101 Lincoln Road, Los Angeles, CA 90014

Education

Belmont High School, Los Angeles 1988-1992

English	4 years
general math	2 years
business math	1 year
typing	2 years
electrical shop	2 years

References

Mrs. Sara Lawson
Petland
24 Hillside Avenue
Los Angeles, CA 90046
(213) 763-7140

Mr. Harold Metz
Guidance Counselor
Belmont High School
Los Angeles, CA 90026
(213) 472-2933

Completing a Job Application

To apply for most jobs, you need to complete a job application. Complete the application on pages 35 and 36. Then keep it and use it as a guide to help you fill out other applications.

1 **Personal Information.** The employer wants to make sure it is legal for you to work in this state. Each state has a law about how old you have to be. You also have to be a United States citizen or have a green card. Your driver's license number tells your employer that you can drive to work. You may need to be able to drive to do this job.

2 **Position.** You are asked how much salary you expect to earn. Don't say you will work for any amount. You will want to consider the company's **benefits,** which are extra items such as health insurance and paid vacation. If the company has poor benefits, you may ask for more salary. If the company has good benefits, you may ask for less salary. The application also asks what hours you are willing to work. Remember your values. Your family needs may be more important to you than this job.

3 **Education.** List any special skills you have. Write down first the ones that will help you do this job.

4 **Military.** If you have not been in the military, put lines in these blanks. Then the employer will know that you did not skip the question. The employer will know that the question did not apply to you. Never skip questions on a job application.

APPLICATION FOR EMPLOYMENT

World Import Company

An Equal Opportunity Employer

1 PERSONAL

LAST NAME	FIRST	MIDDLE	SOCIAL SECURITY NUMBER
HOME STREET ADDRESS			HOME PHONE NO.
CITY	STATE	ZIP	LENGTH OF TIME AT PRESENT ADDRESS:

❑ YES ❑ NO   Are you over the age of 18?   ❑ YES ❑ NO   Are you legally authorized to work in the United States?

❑ YES ❑ NO Do you have a valid driver's license in this state?	License No.
❑ YES ❑ NO Have you ever applied for a position or worked for this company?	If so, when?
❑ YES ❑ NO Do you have any relatives employed by World Import Company?	If so, please name.

2 POSITION

Position Applied For:	Expected Salary:
❑ YES ❑ NO Are you available for work on a full-time basis?	If no, number of hours per week you can work:

❑ YES ❑ NO   Will you work overtime if asked?

How did you learn about our Company?

❑ Store Ad   ❑ Newspaper   ❑ State Employment Office   ❑ Employee   ❑ Other

3 EDUCATION

High School Name and Location	Did you graduate? ❑ Yes ❑ No ❑ GED	Date diploma or equivalent received:	
Other (Trade or Vocational Schools, College,etc.)		Degree	Date of Degree
Special Skills or Training (Languages, Equipment, etc.)			

4 MILITARY

Branch of Service:	Period of Active Duty: From: To:	Rank at Discharge:
Describe Duties or Training:		

5 EXPERIENCE (Last Job First)

Company Name		Dates of Employment (Mo./Yr.)		
		From:	To	
Address		City	State	Zip
Last Position Held	Supervisor	Supervisor's Phone #	Last Salary (Mo./Wk.)	
Reason for Leaving:				

Company Name		Dates of Employment (Mo./Yr.)		
		From:	To:	
Address		City	State	Zip
Last Position Held	Supervisor	Supervisor's Phone #	Last Salary (Mo./Wk.)	
Reason for Leaving:				

Company Name		Dates of Employment (Mo./Yr.)		
		From:	To:	
Address		City	State	Zip
Last Position Held	Supervisor	Supervisor's Phone #	Last Salary (Mo./Wk.)	
Reason for Leaving:				

6 REFERENCES (other than relatives or former employers)

1. Name	Area Code/Phone Number	Occupation	
Street	City	State	Zip
2. Name	Area Code/Phone Number	Occupation	
Street	City	State	Zip
3. Name	Area Code/Phone Number	Occupation	
Street	City	State	Zip

❏ YES ❏ NO	Have you ever been fired, discharged, or asked to resign from any job within the last five years?	If yes, state reason:
❏ YES ❏ NO	Have you been convicted of a crime within the last five years? If yes, give details. (A conviction record will not necessarily bar you from employment.)	

How many days have you been absent
from scheduled work in the past year?

7 STATEMENT

I authorize employers, schools, and references to furnish information in connection with this application. I agree to provide, if employed, authorization to work in the U.S. as required by the Immigration Reform and Control Act. If requested, I agree to submit to a medical examination by a company physician and/or screening for the presence of a prohibited substance. If employed, I agree to comply with this company's rules and policies. I certify that this application was completed by me and that all information is complete and true and that any misrepresentation by me in the application will be sufficient cause for dismissal.

SIGNED: _____ DATE: _____

5 **Experience.** This section asks about your past jobs. Write down the last job first. This application has space for three jobs. Sometimes you will have to list more. Or you may be asked to list all your jobs in the past ten years. Try not to leave any time gaps in your work history. You are also asked why you left each job. Don't say anything about problems you had on your last job. Instead, say something else that is true. You might say that you got a better offer. You could point out that you went back to school. Or perhaps your company moved to another state.

6 **References.** This section asks for references. This company does not want the names of relatives or past employers. Always ask your references if you may use them. Ask if you may give out their telephone number at home or at work. This section also asks if you have been found guilty of any crimes. If yes, you can ask to talk to the employer in private.

7 **Statement.** Your signature means that you agree to let the company check out the information you gave on this form. You also agree to a drug test, if the company wants to test you at any time.

WORKSHOP PRACTICE: Applying for a Job by Phone

You may have to apply for a job by phone. Imagine calling one of the employers from the ads on page 21. Say that you want to apply for a job and ask how to do it. If you are told to come for an interview, ask for the time, date, and place. On the lines below, write five sentences that show what you would say or ask during your phone call.

1. _____

   _____

2. _____

   _____

3. _____

   _____

4. _____

   _____

5. _____

   _____

VOCABULARY: Find the Meaning

On the line write the word or phrase that best completes each sentence.

1. Writing a letter of application is one way to _____ for a job.

   hire   apply   send

2. A neat, well-written letter will make a good _____ on an employer.

   impression   sale   friend

3. The people an employer can call to learn more about you are your

   _____ .

   neighbors   references   counselors

4. A one-page summary that tells about your work experience, education, and skills is called a _____ .

report   letter   resume

5. Employers _____ people when they give them jobs.

sell   hire   see

6. To _____ means to ask for something.

request   experience   send

COMPREHENSION: Finish the Paragraph

Use the following words to finish the paragraph. Write the words you choose on the correct lines.

neatly
religion
in person
application
Help Wanted
race

People often apply for jobs by calling the telephone numbers in the _____ ads. Sometimes people have to go _____ to apply for a job. When you go to see the employer, you need to dress _____ . Other times, you may have to write a letter of _____ that tells why you would be good for the job. It is against the law for an employer to refuse to hire you because of your age, sex, _____ , or _____ .

Thinking and Writing

Think about the kind of job you want. Then write a letter of application to a possible employer. In your letter tell about your education, work experience, and special skills that will help you do a good job. Make your letter look like a business letter. Write your letter on separate paper or in your journal.

CHAPTER 4

YOUR JOB INTERVIEW

THINK ABOUT AS YOU READ

- How do you prepare for a job interview?
- How do you dress for an interview?
- What do you do after your interview?

José Martinez wants to work in a pet store. He applied for a job at a few stores. The owner of one pet store asked José to come for an interview. José is nervous about the interview. He is not sure about what to wear. He does not know what questions to ask the employer. In this chapter you will learn what to say and do for your interviews. A good interview will help you get the job you want.

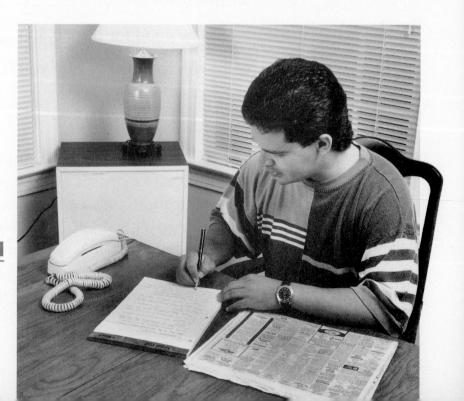

Preparing for an interview can help you get the job.

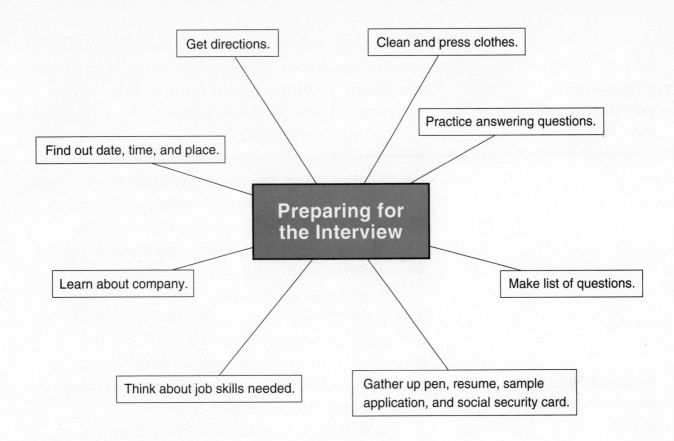

Get directions.

Clean and press clothes.

Practice answering questions.

Find out date, time, and place.

Preparing for the Interview

Learn about company.

Make list of questions.

Think about job skills needed.

Gather up pen, resume, sample application, and social security card.

Preparing for Your Interview

After you apply for a job, you may be asked to come for an interview. You may receive a phone call or a letter inviting you for the interview. Make sure you know the date, the time, and the place. Write down all this information.

Learn as much as you can about the company before you go for your interview. Find out what the company does or makes. Find out about the job you are applying for. Think about the skills you have that will help you in this job.

Find out how to get to the interview. You may need to take a bus or train. Find out which bus or train to take and where to get off. Learn how long the trip will take. Give yourself enough time to travel. Plan to arrive 10 or 15 minutes early to make sure you are not late. Getting there early shows the employer that you really want the job.

The night before you go, prepare what you need to take. You will need your social security card, pen, **sample** job application, and resume. Take your green card if you are not a citizen.

The employer will ask you questions during the interview. Many of the questions will be like the sample questions in the Necessary Skills Workshop on page 48. Practice answering these sample questions before your interview. You may want a friend to interview you with these sample questions. Practice your answers so they are clear and interesting.

You will also have a chance to ask questions. Plan your questions before the interview. Write down five questions that you want to ask the employer. Your questions can be about your job **responsibilities.** They can be about job training, benefits, and company rules.

You will want to look your best for your interview. You may need to get a haircut several days before the interview. You will want to wear the right clothes to your interview. For women, a business dress or suit would be good to wear. Do not use too much jewelry and makeup. For men, a tie and jacket would be fine. Be sure your clothes look clean and pressed. Wear clean shoes that look nice. You want to make a good impression.

Which clothing would make a better impression on an employer?

Dress correctly for your interview.

At the Interview

During the interview, you want to show the employer that you are the right person for the job. The employer may interview a few people. You want to show that you have the education and skills to do the job well.

You will probably meet other people who work for the company when you go for your interview. Be friendly and polite to everyone you meet. Sometimes the employer will ask other workers how they feel about you.

The employer may greet you by shaking your hand. Shake hands **firmly.** Remember the employer's name.

Firmly means strongly.

You want to make a good impression during the interview. Speak clearly and use correct English. Look at the employer's face when you speak. Take your time to answer questions completely, but do not talk too much. Do not say anything bad about your last employer. In your answers show that you have the skills to do the job well.

To be **confident** means to be sure of yourself and your skills.

Your interest in the job is also important in a job interview. Show the employer that you really want the job. Sit up straight and tall. Act **confident.** Be pleasant. The employer wants to see that you would get along well with other workers.

At the end of the interview, the employer will give you time to ask questions. This is the time to ask the questions you prepared at home. Do not ask questions that the employer has already given you information about. The chart on page 45 tells you what to do and not do during an interview.

The employer may not make a decision about hiring you during the interview. At the end of the interview, ask the employer when a decision will be made. Ask who you can call and when. Try to get some firm answers. You want to follow up on your interview with another visit or telephone call. Before you leave, shake hands and thank the employer for the interview.

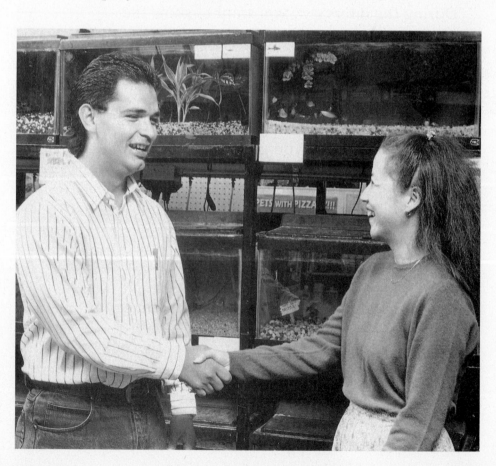

A good interview is important to getting a good job.

Things to Do and Not Do for a Job Interview

Do

1. Look clean and neat.
2. Come alone.
3. Come early.
4. Wear clean, pressed business clothes.
5. Practice answering questions at home that you think you will be asked.
6. Bring a list of questions to ask the employer about the job.
7. Bring a pen, a resume, your Social Security card, and a completed sample job application.
8. Look straight at the employer's face when you speak.
9. Tell how your skills will help you do the job well.
10. Explain your ideas and opinions.

Don't

1. Don't come looking dirty and messy.
2. Don't bring a friend.
3. Don't come late.
4. Don't wear dirty clothes or wrinkled clothes.
5. Don't talk too much at the interview.
6. Don't ask too many questions about lunch, breaks, and vacations.
7. Don't chew gum, smoke, or show nervous habits.
8. Don't look down when you speak.
9. Don't talk about your personal problems.
10. Don't talk badly about your past employers.

After the Interview

Always write a thank-you letter to the person who interviewed you. Your letter may help the employer decide to hire you. Look at the letter on page 47. José wrote it the day after an interview. A thank-you letter is **brief.** Make sure it is neatly written with correct spelling. Make your thank-you letter look like a business letter.

Perhaps you will not get the job that you were interviewed for. You can ask if there are any other jobs at this company you can apply for. You can also ask if the employer knows about other job leads at other companies.

You may go for many interviews before you are hired for a job. Never give up. Keep applying for jobs. Go for more interviews. Practice your questions and answers before each interview. Always look your best. One day you will be told that you have been hired for the job.

To be **brief** means to be short in time or in length.

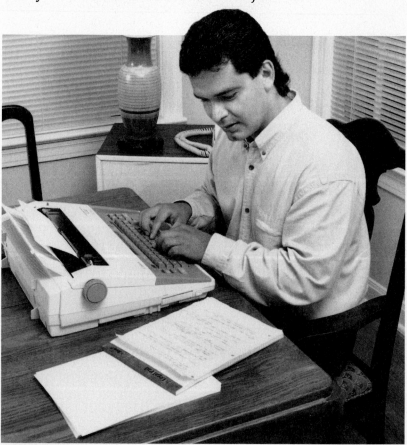

Follow up your interview with a thank-you letter.

22 Maple Street
Los Angeles, CA 90046
February 8, 1994

Mr. Allen Mills
Pets Unlimited
175 W. 9th Street
Los Angeles, CA 90015

Dear Mr. Mills:

   Thank you for giving me a job interview on Monday, February 7, 1994.

   I know I would enjoy working at your pet store. My experience in caring for animals in other pet stores will help me do a good job for you.

   I will give you a call Friday to find out your decision. Or feel free to call me before then. I can be reached at 375-2865 after 4:00 p.m.

                                        Sincerely,

                                        José Martinez

                                        José Martinez

Your Job Interview

Every employer wants to hire workers who have the right skills to do a good job. They also want workers who have pleasant personalities. So most employers ask the same kind of questions during an interview.

Below are 15 common interview questions. You will probably be asked many of these questions during your interview. Read each question. Then write your answer on a separate sheet of paper or in your journal. You may want to practice with a partner.

1. What can you tell about yourself?
2. What do you like to do in your free time?
3. Do you want a permanent job or a temporary job?
4. Why do you want this job?
5. What are your career goals? How will this job help you meet those goals?
6. What special skills do you have for the job?
7. Why do you think you would do a better job for this company than another person?
8. What do you know about this company?
9. How long do you think you would want to work for this company?
10. Are you working now? If you are now working, what job do you have? Why do you want to leave?
11. Why did you leave your last job?
12. What did you enjoy most about your last job?
13. What didn't you like about your last job?
14. Do you have any problems or disabilities that would prevent you from doing this job?
15. What do you want for a starting salary?

Questions You Want to Ask

You will have time to ask questions during your interview. Think of five questions you would like to ask the employer. Write your questions on a separate sheet of paper or in your journal.

WORKSHOP PRACTICE: Prepare for a Job Interview
Imagine that you have a job interview next week. You want to make a good impression on the employer. So you want to prepare for the interview. List six things you would do to prepare for your interview.

1. _____

_____

2. _____

_____

3. _____

_____

4. _____

_____

5. _____

_____

6. _____

_____

VOCABULARY: Writing with Vocabulary Words
Use six or more of the following words or phrases to write a paragraph that tells what to do for a job interview.

responsibilities
sample
employer
resume
confident
hire
education
brief
firmly

_____

_____

_____

_____

_____

_____

COMPREHENSION: Circle the Answer
Draw a circle around the correct answer.

1. What do you need to know when going for an interview?

   date, time, and place

   nearest library

   closest bakery

2. What is a good time to arrive for the interview?

   a few minutes late

   30 minutes early

   10 to 15 minutes early

3. What is the wrong thing to do during an interview?

   look at the employer when speaking

   tell about your work experience

   talk about personal problems

4. What is a good question to ask the employer?

   What time is lunch?

   What responsibilities will I have?

   How many breaks will I get?

5. When should you write a thank-you letter after an interview?

   the next day

   two weeks later

   one month later

Thinking and Writing

Practice writing a thank-you letter to an employer. Look back at José's letter on page 47. Then write your letter to look like a business letter. Write your letter on separate paper or in your journal.

CHAPTER 5

GETTING TO WORK

THINK ABOUT AS YOU READ

- What are the different ways you can get to work?
- Why is it important to use bus and train schedules?
- How can you plan your own schedule so you can be at work on time?

When Laura started her new job, she wanted her employer to be happy with her work. Being late for work is one reason some people lose their jobs. Laura decided that she would try to be on time every day. She lives far from her job, but she is always on time. In this chapter you will learn what you can do to get to work on time.

Getting to work on time takes planning.

Traveling to Work

You may live so close to your job that you can walk to work. You will be getting good exercise. You will also save money because you will not be paying for **transportation.**

If you want to walk to work, you need to know how much time it will take you. Then leave for work early enough so that you can walk to your job and be on time. For example, perhaps you have to be at work at 7:00 A.M. You know it will take you twenty minutes to walk to your job. Leave your home at 6:35 A.M. That is 25 minutes before 7:00 A.M. You will be five minutes early when you get to your job at 6:55 A.M.

You may be one of the millions of people who cannot walk to work. You may want to drive your own car to work. Then you will need to learn which roads to take. Find out how much time the trip will take. Allow some extra time for traffic problems. Allow more time for driving in bad weather.

You will need to find out where you can park your car. You may have to pay for parking. This can be very expensive.

Transportation means different ways to travel, such as by cars, trains, and buses.

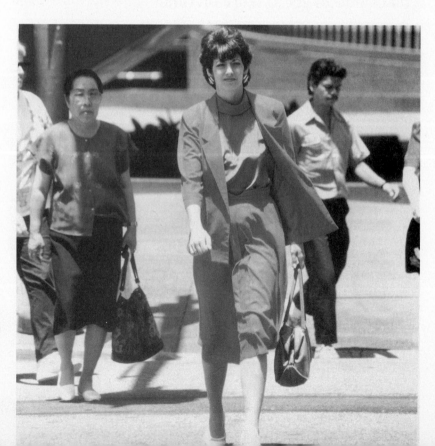

Walking to work is good exercise.

52

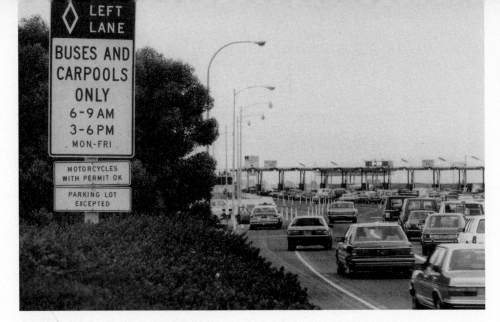

Riding in a car-pool can save money.

Owning a car is expensive. Car repairs, insurance, and gas cost very much. You can save money by forming a **car-pool.** To form a car-pool, you need a few people who live and work near each other. Then you can travel together to work. All people in the car-pool share the cost of gas, **tolls**, and parking fees.

Many people travel by train to work. Some large cities have subway trains that run under the city streets. These trains are not expensive, and they move fast.

Other people use **commuter trains** to travel from one city to another. These trains run on a **schedule.** Check the train schedule to know which train to take and how long the ride will be.

Plan which train to take so you can be on time. Perhaps you have to be at work at 7:00 A.M. You have learned that the train ride takes 45 minutes. The train schedule shows that there is a train you can take at 6:00 A.M. It will arrive at the station near your job at 6:45 A.M. From the train station, you will have a short walk to your job. You arrive at work a few minutes before 7:00 A.M.

In many parts of the nation, people use buses to travel to work. To travel by bus, find out if there is a bus stop near your job. Find out if the bus near your job takes a route that stops near your home.

A **car-pool** is a group of people who travel in one car so that they do not have to drive separate cars to the same place.

Tolls are the money you pay for the use of some bridges, tunnels, and highways.

Commuter trains are trains that carry people from one city to another.

A **schedule** is a plan for getting things done or being at a certain place at a certain time.

Plan for rush-hour crowds in your workday schedule.

A **transfer** is a ticket that allows you to ride on a second bus without having to pay a second time.

A **fare** is the money you pay to ride in a bus, train, plane, or taxi.

You may need to take more than one bus to get to work. The bus near your home may not stop near your job. Then you have to take the bus near your home to a bus that will stop near your job. You may get a **transfer** on the first bus. Use that transfer to take the second bus. By using the transfer, you will not have to pay another bus **fare**.

Many buses run on a schedule. At certain times the bus will run often. At other times the bus may run only once an hour. It is important to read the bus schedule. Find out when the bus will arrive at your bus stop. Learn how long the bus ride to work will take.

Planning a Workday Schedule

To be at work on time, you need to know how long it takes you to get ready in the morning. You need to know how long your trip to work will take. When you know how long it takes you to get ready and to travel, you will know how early you need to get up each morning.

Plan a workday schedule for yourself. Think about what you need to do before you leave for work. Make a list. You have to get dressed and eat breakfast. You may want to take a shower and pack a lunch. Think about how much time you will need for each thing on your list. Then you will be able to do everything on your list and be on time for work.

Include time in your schedule for getting to work. Check the bus or train schedule. These schedules will tell you how much time your ride will take. Then add time for getting to the bus or train. Add time for getting from the bus or train to your job. Then you will know which bus or train to take.

Laura made this schedule for herself. She has to be at work at 8:00 A.M.

Laura's Schedule	
5:45 A.M.	Wake up when the alarm clock rings.
5:50 A.M.	Take a shower.
6:10 A.M.	Prepare and eat breakfast.
6:35 A.M.	Pack a lunch.
6:45 A.M.	Get dressed.
7:00 A.M.	Leave for work. Walk to the bus stop.
7:10 A.M.	Wait for the bus for five minutes.
7:15 A.M.	Ride thirty minutes on the bus to work.
7:45 A.M.	Get off the bus. Walk five minutes to the job.
7:50 A.M.	Arrive at work ten minutes early.

Plan a schedule for yourself. Include time for eating and dressing. Include enough time for traveling to work. Practice your schedule once before starting your new job. You may need to change your schedule. You may find you need more time or less time for certain parts of your schedule.

Getting to work on time is an important goal. To meet your goal, learn the best way to get to work. Then learn how much time you will need for your trip. Plan your own schedule to help you use your time well. Being on time will help you keep your job.

Reading a Bus Schedule

Look at the bus schedule on the next page. Notice the following parts.

1 The left side of the bus schedule shows the bus route from Park Avenue to Lakeview Road. This is the weekday schedule. The Saturday and Sunday schedules may be different.

2 The right side of the schedule shows the route going the other way. It goes from Lakeview Road to Park Avenue.

3 The key shows that some buses have a wheelchair lift. The key also shows that morning times (A.M.) are in dark print on this schedule.

4 Suppose you live at Park Avenue and work at Mott Street. You have to be at work at 7:00 A.M. The bus arrives at Mott Street at 6:50 A.M. You would have to catch the bus at 6:35 A.M. at Park Avenue to get to work on time. Your ride would be from 6:35 until 6:50, or 15 minutes long. (6:50 – 6:35 = 15 minutes)

■ ■ ■

Use the schedule to answer the following questions.

1. Bill lives on Woods Avenue. His new job is five minutes from the Lakeview Road stop. Bill must be at work at 8:30 A.M. Bill needs to take the bus that stops at Lakeview Road at what time? _____

2. To be at work at 8:30 A.M., Bill needs to get on the bus at the Woods Avenue stop at what time? _____

3. Bill's ride to work should take about _____ minutes.

4. Bill leaves work at 5:30 P.M. The earliest bus he can catch at the Lakeview Road stop leaves at what time? _____

5. Bill should reach his stop at Woods Avenue at what time? _____

6. A person with a wheelchair wants to get on the bus at Park Avenue to be at Riverside Drive by 10:30 A.M. That person needs to get on the bus at what time? _____

Park Ave. to Lakeview Rd.
WEEKDAYS

Park Ave.	Woods Ave.	Mott St.	Riverside Dr.	Lakeview Rd.
5	4	3	2	1
6:05	6:16	6:19	6:21	6:29 ♿
6:35	6:47	6:50	6:53	7:02
7:09	7:21	7:24	7:27	7:36
—	7:48	7:51	7:54	8:03 ♿
7:39	7:51	7:54	7:57	8:06 ♿
8:09	8:21	8:24	8:27	8:36
8:39	8:51	8:54	8:56	9:04 ♿
9:06	9:17	9:20	9:22	9:30
9:35	9:46	9:49	9:51	9:59
10:05	10:16	10:19	10:21	10:29 ♿
10:35	10:46	10:49	10:51	10:59
11:05	11:16	11:19	11:21	11:29
11:35	11:46	11:49	11:51	11:59
12:05	12:16	12:19	12:21	12:29
12:35	12:46	12:49	12:51	12:59
1:05	1:16	1:19	1:21	1:29
1:35	1:46	1:49	1:51	1:59 ♿
2:05	2:16	2:19	2:21	2:29
2:35	2:46	2:49	2:51	2:59 ♿
3:05	3:16	3:19	3:21	3:29
3:37	3:49	3:53	3:56	4:05
4:10	4:22	4:26	4:29	4:38
4:40	4:52	4:56	4:59	5:08
5:10	5:22	5:26	5:29	5:38 ♿
5:40	5:51	5:54	5:56	6:04
6:06	6:17	6:20	6:22	6:30
6:36	6:47	6:50	6:52	7:00
7:05	7:16	7:19	7:21	7:29 ♿
7:35	7:46	7:49	7:51	7:59
8:05	8:16	8:19	8:21	8:29
9:05	9:16	9:19	9:21	9:29 ♿
10:05	10:16	10:19	10:21	10:29

Lakeview Rd. to Park Ave.
WEEKDAYS

Lakeview Rd.	Riverside Dr.	Mott St.	Woods Ave.	Park Ave.
1	2	3	4	5
6:10	6:19	6:21	6:24	6:35 ♿
6:40	6:50	6:53	6:57	7:09
7:10	7:20	7:23	7:27	7:39
7:40	7:50	7:53	7:57	8:09 ♿
8:10	8:20	8:23	8:27	8:39 ♿
8:40	8:50	8:52	8:55	9:06
9:10	9:19	9:21	9:24	9:35 ♿
9:40	9:49	9:51	9:54	10:05
10:10	10:19	10:21	10:24	10:35
10:40	10:49	10:51	10:54	11:05 ♿
11:10	11:19	11:21	11:24	11:35
11:40	11:49	11:51	11:54	12:05
12:10	12:19	12:21	12:24	12:35
12:40	12:49	12:51	12:54	1:05
1:10	1:19	1:21	1:24	1:35
1:40	1:49	1:51	1:54	2:05
2:10	2:19	2:21	2:24	2:35 ♿
2:40	2:49	2:51	2:54	3:05
3:10	3:19	3:21	3:24	3:37 ♿
3:30	3:40	3:43	3:47	—
3:40	3:50	3:53	3:57	4:10
4:10	4:20	4:23	4:27	4:40
4:40	4:50	4:53	4:57	5:10
5:10	5:20	5:23	5:27	5:40 ♿
5:40	5:49	5:51	5:54	6:05
6:10	6:19	6:21	6:24	6:35
6:40	6:49	6:51	6:54	7:05
7:10	7:19	7:21	7:24	7:35 ♿
7:40	7:49	7:51	7:54	8:05
8:10	8:19	8:21	8:24	8:35
8:40	8:49	8:51	8:54	9:05 ♿
9:40	9:49	9:51	9:54	10:05

Key
♿ = wheelchair lift
Dark print shows A.M.

WORKSHOP PRACTICE: Plan Your Schedule

Planning your own schedule can help you get to work on time. In the space below, plan how much time you need to get to work and to take care of your needs at home. Write down the times that you think you need to do everything on your list. You may want to look back at Laura's schedule on page 55. Keep this schedule and try to follow it.

Need to Do	Time
Wake up	_____
Take a shower	_____
Get dressed	_____
Cook and eat breakfast	_____
Pack lunch	_____
Other _____	_____
Other _____	_____
Leave for work	_____
Travel to work	_____
Arrive at work	_____
Start work	_____

VOCABULARY: Find the Meaning

On the line write the word or phrase that best completes each sentence.

1. You will not have to pay to go on a second bus if you get a

   _____ .

   fare   schedule   transfer

2. The different ways people travel are called _____ .

   tolls   transportation   fares

3. The money you pay to travel on a plane, bus, or train is the

_____ .

fare   resume   occupation

4. The money you pay to use certain bridges, highways, and tunnels is

called a _____ .

fare   toll   transfer

5. A group of people who travel in the same car instead of driving

separate cars is called a _____ .

transportation   car-pool   transfer

COMPREHENSION: True or False

Write True next to each sentence that is true. Write False next to each sentence that is false. There are two false sentences.

_____ **1.** You can take a train that arrives five minutes from your job at 7:45 A.M. and be at work before 8:00 A.M.

_____ **2.** You need thirty minutes to ride to work and your job starts at 8:00 A.M., so you can wake up at 7:30 A.M.

_____ **3.** Getting to work on time is important to your job.

_____ **4.** A schedule can help you get to work on time.

_____ **5.** It is less expensive to drive your own car to work than to be in a car-pool.

On the lines that follow, rewrite the two false sentences to make them true.

_____

_____

Thinking and Writing

Imagine you are starting a new job. Your working hours will be 11:00 P.M. to 7:00 A.M. You have never worked at night before. You will need time for sleeping, eating, chores, and fun. If you have family, you will need time for them. How can you plan your schedule so you can get to work on time? Explain your new schedule in your journal.

KEEPING YOUR JOB

Sharon Kane followed all the right steps to find a job. After an interview, she was hired to work in a factory. Sharon wants her employer to like her work. She wants the other workers to like her. Sharon wants to keep her job. As you read this chapter, you will learn ways to keep your job.

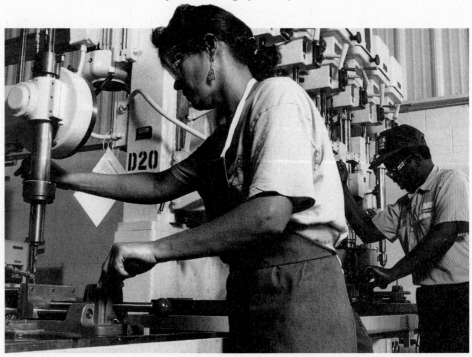

Learn how to do your job correctly.

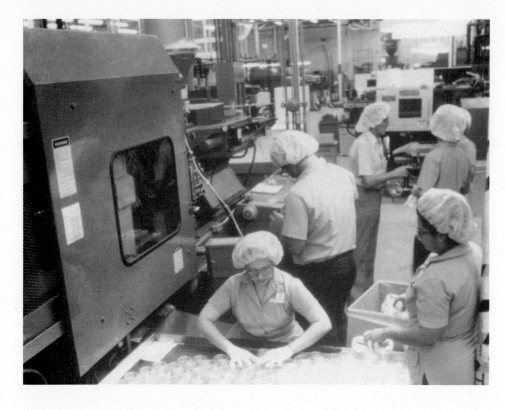

Follow company rules on the job.

The First Day on the Job

You may feel nervous about starting your new job. You want to start your job the right way. By following these steps, you can get off to a good start.

1. Be on time. Plan to arrive ten minutes early.

2. Find out your **supervisor's** name.

3. Introduce yourself to your **co-workers**.

4. Fill out any forms that your employer gives you.

5. Learn your job responsibilities.

6. Find out when and where to have lunch and breaks.

7. Be pleasant.

How to Keep Your Job

There are many things you can do to keep your job. Come to work on time. Be a good worker. Always do your share of the work.

Your **supervisor** is the person who is your boss.

Co-workers are people who work with you.

A **manual** is a book that has the company's rules for its workers. It may also have directions for workers about how to use machines and tools.

Always follow your company's rules. Many companies have their own **manuals.** These manuals have rules and directions for workers. As a new worker, you may be told to study the manual. Read it carefully. Ask your supervisor to explain the rules that you do not understand. Try hard to follow all rules and directions.

Your appearance can help you keep your job. It is important to wear the right kind of clothes for your job. Jeans and safety boots may be right for factory work or outdoor jobs. A man may wear a tie and jacket for an office job. Make sure your clothes are always clean and pressed.

Getting along with your co-workers will help you keep your job. It is also important to get along with your supervisors. Try hard not to fight or argue with people at work. Do not talk about co-workers and supervisors.

Alcohol is found in wine, beer, and liquor. It changes the way the brain thinks and works.

Employers do not want workers to use drugs or **alcohol.** Workers cannot think clearly when they use drugs or alcohol. They can get into accidents. They cannot do their best work. Staying away from drugs and alcohol will help you keep your job.

How You Can Lose Your Job

Some workers lose their jobs because of poor work and poor behavior. Some of the reasons workers lose their jobs are listed below.

1. Being late too many times.

2. Leaving work early without permission.

3. Not following company rules.

4. Not getting along with co-workers, supervisors, or customers.

5. Being absent too many days.

6. Stealing money or supplies from the company.

7. Spending too much time at lunch and on breaks.

8. Making too many mistakes.

9. Using company phones for personal calls.

10. Not doing a good job.

Collecting Unemployment Insurance

Even good workers sometimes lose their jobs. This can happen if the company is not earning enough money. Then the company will need fewer workers.

Laid off means you lose your job because the employer needs fewer workers.

Unemployment insurance is insurance for workers who lose their jobs.

A **benefit** is the money that an insurance company pays a worker.

A **stub** is the paper attached to a paycheck. It has salary information.

Workers' compensation is insurance that pays medical bills of people who get hurt while working. It may pay part of the salary to a worker who gets hurt and cannot work.

Good workers may be **laid off** in order to save money. They may be laid off if their company needs fewer workers. Most employers pay unemployment taxes for all of their workers. Workers may be able to get money from **unemployment insurance** if they get laid off.

If you get laid off, you may be able to collect **benefits** from unemployment insurance. If you have worked for the company a certain amount of time, you may be able to collect benefits. If you quit or if you are fired, you may not be able to collect benefits. These are the rules in most states. The rules in your state may be different. Check with your state's unemployment office to find out the rules in your state.

If you lose your job, go to your state's unemployment office. Find out where there is an office near your home. Bring your social security card and a **stub** from one of your last paychecks. Also bring the name and address of your last employer. Bring a W-2 form if you have one. You will get a W-2 form from your employer in January. It shows how much you earned the past year. It shows how much federal income tax you paid.

You will fill out an application for unemployment benefits at the office. Within a few weeks, you may receive benefits. In most states to get benefits you will have to look for work each week. Each state has its own rules about how long and how much you can collect.

Collecting Workers' Compensation

What do you need to do if you get hurt or sick while working? Tell your employer at once. You may be able to receive benefits from **workers' compensation** insurance.

In most states employers pay for workers' compensation insurance for their workers. In some states workers also pay part of the insurance cost.

Workers' compensation insurance pays benefits if you are hurt while doing your job. It may pay your hospital and medical bills. It may pay part of your salary until you are able to return to work.

You cannot collect workers' compensation benefits unless you tell your employer you were hurt. Your employer fills out forms that explain how you were hurt. Each state has its own rules about workers' compensation. If you get hurt or sick while working, find out the rules from the workers' compensation office in your state.

Once you start your job, you will want to keep it. Always being on time, following safety rules, and doing good work will help you keep your job. If you are laid off, you may be able to collect unemployment insurance. If you are hurt on the job, you may be able to collect workers' compensation.

Reading a Safety Manual

Many employers give their workers, or **employees,** a manual containing company rules. Workers are expected to read and obey the rules in the manual. Following are some safety rules from the American Public Power Association's safety manual. Read these rules from the manual. Note that in a manual the word *shall* is a command.

1. All employees shall carefully study these safety rules that apply to their duties. Obeying these safety rules is a requirement for employment.

2. Before beginning a job, employees shall be sure they can perform the job without being hurt. Before beginning a job, employees shall understand the work to be done and the safety rules which apply.

3. Injuries, no matter how slight, shall be reported to the person in charge as soon as possible.

4. Before beginning any work that may be dangerous, employees shall take care to use safe procedures. Safety is always more important than speed.

5. Employees shall not participate in practical jokes.

6. Warning signs shall be obeyed. People who are seen in dangerous situations shall be warned.

7. Use of alcohol or drugs by employees is not allowed. Employees taking drugs prescribed by a physician or over-the-counter drugs which could affect their work shall report the fact to their supervisors.

8. Both the inside and outside of buildings shall be kept clean at all times.

9. No clothing shall be allowed to hang on walls or behind doors. No matches shall be left in clothes placed in lockers.

10. All "No Smoking" signs shall be obeyed.

11. Smoking shall not be permitted in storerooms, battery rooms, or in other areas where dangerous materials are kept. Smoking is not allowed in dangerous places even if "No Smoking" signs are missing.

12. Fire protection equipment shall be properly located at all times.

13. All employees shall always wear clothing and shoes which are suitable for the work they are doing.

14. Loose chains, key chains, or unnecessary metal of any kind shall not be worn when working on or near electricity.

■ ■ ■

Write answers to the questions about the rules in the manual.

1. What must all employees read and obey? (See Rule 1.)

   _____

2. What shall workers do about injuries? (See Rule 3.)

   _____

3. Are practical jokes allowed? (See Rule 5.)

   _____

4. What are the rules about drugs and alcohol? (See Rule 7.)

   _____

   _____

5. Where are workers not allowed to hang clothing? (See Rule 9.)

   _____

6. Where are workers not allowed to smoke? (See Rule 11.)

   _____

7. What are workers not allowed to wear when working near electricity?

   (See Rule 14.) _____

WORKSHOP PRACTICE: Following Safety Rules

Look at the rules from the safety manual again. Below you will read about some workers who did not obey these safety rules. Write the number of the rule each worker needed to read and obey.

_____ 1. Bob was smoking in the storeroom.

_____ 2. Joe put lemon in Bob's coffee.

_____ 3. Cecilia decided to skip a safety step to get the job done faster.

_____ 4. Rafael had a few beers with his lunch.

_____ 5. Carmen sprained her wrist but did not tell anyone.

_____ 6. Bennie wore tennis shoes instead of safety boots.

_____ 7. Marie hung her coat on the door.

_____ 8. Pat left matches in a jacket and put it in a locker.

VOCABULARY: Finish the Sentence

Choose one of the following words or phrases to complete each sentence. Write the word or phrase on the correct line.

supervisors
co-workers
manual
alcohol
benefit
laid off

1. When you lose your job because your employer no longer needs you, you are _____ .

2. The money that you receive from insurance is called a _____ .

3. Beer, liquor, and wine are drinks that contain _____ .

4. People who act as the bosses are _____ .

5. The rules of a company are often in its _____ .

6. The people you work with are your _____ .

COMPREHENSION: Circle the Answer

Draw a circle around the correct answer.

1. What can cause you to lose your job?

   stealing supplies

   obeying company rules

   doing your share of the work

2. For which job would workers wear jeans and safety boots?

   bank work

   factory work

   office work

3. How do drugs and alcohol affect workers?

   They help cause accidents.

   They help them think clearly.

   They help them do excellent work.

4. What kind of benefits can workers collect if they are laid off?

   workers' compensation

   health insurance

   unemployment insurance

5. What kind of benefits can workers collect if they are hurt while working?

   workers' compensation

   vacation money

   unemployment insurance

Thinking and Writing

Imagine that you are an employer. What would cause you to fire a worker? Give at least four reasons. Explain why you would fire a worker for these reasons. Write your answers in your journal.

CHAPTER 7

SUCCESS AT WORK

THINK ABOUT AS YOU READ

- How does getting along with others help you succeed?
- What can you do to get along with others?
- What can you do to get a raise or a promotion?

Lauren Li enjoys working in the department store warehouse. She has been working there for a few weeks. She wants to be **successful** at her job. Lauren hopes to earn a raise. Perhaps one day she will earn a **promotion** to a better job. In this chapter you will learn what you can do to be successful at your job.

You are **successful** if you do something well.

A **promotion** is getting a better-paying job with more responsibilities for the same company.

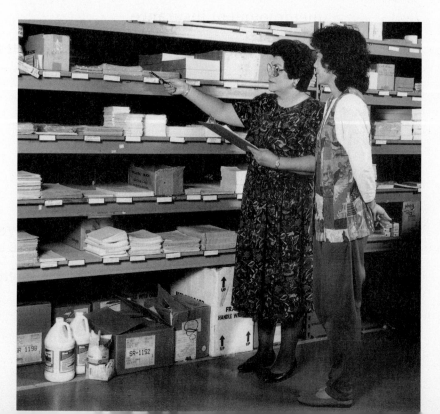

Learn how to do your job well to have success at work.

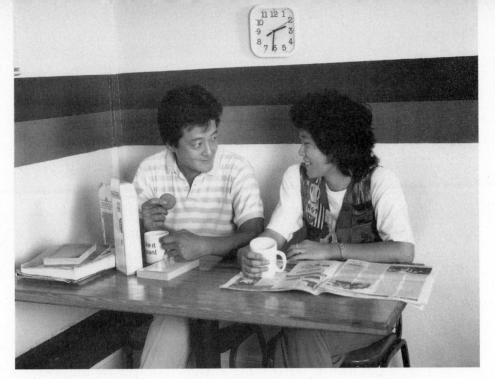

It is important to get along well with your co-workers.

Working Well with Co-workers

Many workers lose their jobs because they do not get along with others. Learning to get along with others will help you succeed. By getting along, you help others do their job well.

You need to show that you are an **independent** worker. Ask for instructions while you are learning your job. Learn your job so that you can do it by yourself. Then you can do your work without being told what to do all the time. Show your co-workers that they can depend on you to do your share of the work.

Be **cooperative.** Show that you can work with a co-worker to get a job done. Help new workers learn their jobs. Learn how to give workers directions that are easy to follow.

Be willing to **compromise.** When two people compromise, each person gives in a little. Lauren compromised with a co-worker about choosing a time for an afternoon break. Lauren wanted her break to be at 2:00 P.M. The co-worker wanted to take a break at 3:00 P.M. They compromised by choosing 2:30 as the time for their break.

You are an **independent** worker if you can work by yourself without asking for help all the time.

A **cooperative** person wants to work together with other people.

To **compromise** means to reach an agreement by having each side give up some of its demands.

71

To **gossip** means to talk about people when they are not there.

Your **attitude** is the feelings and behavior you show about other people or ideas.

If you know how to compromise, you will avoid getting into fights. Fights can cause accidents. You can be fired for fighting or arguing.

Think about the feelings of others. Try not to complain. When you complain, you make things less pleasant for others. Do not **gossip** about your co-workers or supervisor. They will find out what you said. They will be angry with you. Then it will be harder to get along with them.

Working Well with Your Supervisor

To be successful at your job, you will need to get along with your supervisor. Your **attitude** will help you get along with your supervisor. Show a good attitude at work by following these guidelines.

1. Show respect for the ideas and feelings of others. Get along with your co-workers. Be a pleasant person to work with. Treat all people fairly.

2. Be a dependable worker. Be on time. Do not take long breaks. Do your share of the work. Do your job well.

Show that you are an independent worker.

72

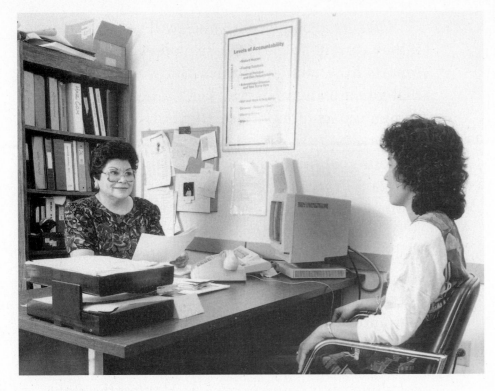

Your supervisor will discuss your work with you. If you do your work well, you may get a raise.

3. Follow all safety rules. Keep your work area clean and safe. Make safety important to you.

4. Accept **criticism** and learn from it. Your supervisor may find fault with your work. You may be told ways to do a better job. Some workers get very angry when they are **criticized.** They may argue or fight with their supervisor. To be successful, listen and learn from criticism. Do not argue or curse. Try to remember that you may not always be right.

A **criticism** is a statement that finds fault with something you do.

You are **criticized** when other people find fault with you.

5. Learn from your mistakes. It is all right to make mistakes. It is not all right to keep making the same ones over and over again.

Getting a Raise and a Promotion

Every worker wants to earn more money. You will earn more money when you get a raise.

Many workers get a raise if they stay at their job for a certain amount of time. Your company may give workers a raise once a year or once in two years.

Workers at some companies will get a raise only if they earn it. To earn a raise, you need good reports from your supervisor. Show your supervisor that you are an honest worker. Work hard for the company. Get along well with your supervisor and co-workers.

Your goal might be to get a promotion with your company. You will get a better salary if you get a promotion. You will also have more responsibilities.

To earn a promotion, you will need to get along well with co-workers and supervisors. You may need to do extra work for the company. You may need to get job training. Job training will help you learn how to do a more difficult job.

To be successful at your job, you will need to work well with your co-workers. You will need to get along with your supervisor. Having the right attitude and working hard will help you get ahead at your job.

Success at Work

Working Well with Co-workers
- Be independent.
- Be cooperative.
- Be willing to compromise.
  - Don't fight.
  - Don't argue.
- Be thoughtful of others.
  - Don't complain.
  - Don't gossip.

Working Well with Supervisor
- Show respect.
- Be dependable.
- Follow safety rules.
- Accept criticism.
- Learn from mistakes.

Getting Along with Others at Work

To be successful at work, you need to get along with workers and supervisors. As a new worker, Lauren Li had two problems. Read each problem. Then write a short paragraph to explain how Lauren should handle the problem.

Problem No. 1. Lauren's job is to pack dishes in boxes. She works slowly to avoid breaking dishes. She often stops to talk to other workers. Lauren leaves many papers on the floor as she works. Her supervisor criticized her for talking too much and working too slowly. The supervisor said leaving papers on the floor is not safe. Now Lauren is angry with the supervisor. What should she do?

_____

_____

_____

_____

_____

_____

Problem No. 2. Lauren had to staple the boxes after she packed the dishes in them. She forgot how to do it the way her supervisor showed her. So she asked other workers to do it for her. One of the workers complained to the supervisor. The supervisor criticized Lauren. Lauren felt very angry. What did Lauren do wrong? How can she correct the problem?

_____

_____

_____

_____

_____

WORKSHOP PRACTICE: Getting a Raise or Promotion

After you have worked at the same job for a while, you may want to get a raise or a promotion. Put a check mark next to each sentence that tells how to get a raise or a promotion. Check four sentences in all.

_____ 1. Be an honest worker.

_____ 2. Get good reports from your supervisor.

_____ 3. Ask for help all the time.

_____ 4. Go for job training to learn how to do more difficult work.

_____ 5. Complain about the job you have now.

_____ 6. Do extra work for the company.

_____ 7. Take long breaks.

VOCABULARY: Matching

Match the word in Group B with a definition in Group A. Write the letter of the correct answer on the line.

Group A

_____ 1. The feelings and behavior you show about other people is called this.

_____ 2. This means to reach an agreement by giving in a little.

_____ 3. You are this kind of worker if you can work by yourself without getting help all the time.

_____ 4. Getting a better job in the same company is called this.

_____ 5. This kind of person wants to work well with others.

_____ 6. This is a statement that finds fault with something you do.

Group B

a. promotion

b. cooperative

c. attitude

d. criticism

e. compromise

f. independent

COMPREHENSION: Finish the Paragraph

Use the following words to finish the paragraph.
Write the words you choose on the correct lines.

promotion
safety
succeed
mistakes
raise
compromise
criticism
cooperative

Being a dependable and _____ worker will help you succeed at work. Having the right attitude can also help you _____ at your job. Learn to accept _____ from supervisors. When you do something wrong, be willing to learn from your _____ . Your supervisor wants you to obey all _____ rules. To get along with other workers, sometimes you may have to give in a little and _____ . If you are a good worker, you may earn a _____ in salary. If you get job training, you may even get a _____ to a better job.

Thinking and Writing

Most people dislike being criticized by their supervisor at work. Write about the right way and the wrong way to act when criticized. Explain why you can be successful at work if you act the right way when criticized. Use your journal or the lines below.

_____

_____

_____

_____

_____

_____

CHAPTER 8

YOUR PAYCHECK AND BENEFITS

THINK ABOUT AS YOU READ

- What deductions are taken out of your paycheck?
- What kinds of taxes do you have to pay?
- What kinds of benefits do you receive?

Your **gross salary** is the full amount of money you earn during a pay period.

Adam Waters started a job as a hospital worker. His salary was $18,000 a year. He was told that he would be paid twice a month. His **gross salary** for the pay period would be $750. But when Adam received his first paycheck, it was for much less than $750. Money had been taken out of his salary

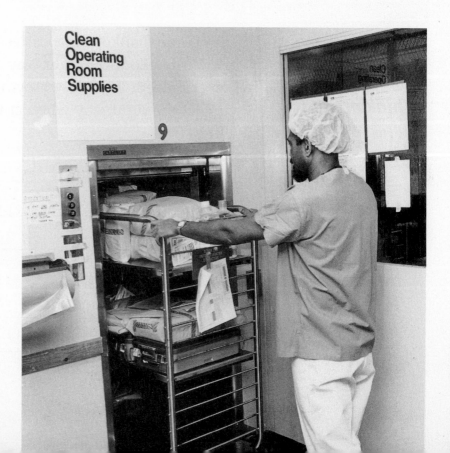

for taxes and other **deductions.** In this chapter you will learn why money is taken out of your salary. You will also learn about some of the **benefits** you may get from your job.

Your Paycheck Stub

You get paid at the end of a pay period. That pay period may be one week, two weeks, or a month. For some workers the pay periods are twice a month. The diagram below shows what gross salaries would be for an $18,000 salary during different pay periods.

For a salary of $18,000 a year, a worker may receive

$346.15 each week
($18,000 ÷ 52 weeks in a year) **or** $692.30 every other week
($18,000 ÷ 26 weeks per year)

or $750 twice a month
($18,000 ÷ 24 times per year) **or** $1,500 once a month
($18,000 ÷ 12 months in a year)

You receive a paycheck for each pay period. A paycheck has two parts. One part is a check. The check will be your **net pay** for the pay period. You can cash your check at your bank.

The second part of your paycheck is the stub. It has information about your salary for each pay period. It shows how much money was taken out for taxes and other deductions. Your paycheck stub shows why your net pay is less than your gross salary. Keep all stubs for your tax records.

One of Adam's paychecks is on page 80. He is paid on the first and fifteenth of each month. There is much detailed information on a paycheck stub. If you have any questions about your paycheck and stub, ask your supervisor or your payroll officer.

Your **net pay** is the amount of money you can keep from your salary.

						TAXES/DED	YEAR TO DATE
WATERS, ADAM 111-22-3333					FEDERAL	68 00	156 00
					FICA/MED	68 85	183 61
DESCRIPTION	RATE	HOURS	EARNINGS	YEAR TO DATE	PENNSYLVANIA	25 20	67 20
					✓ DISABILITY	1 35	3 61
REGULAR EARN	8 65	86 70	749 96	2249 87	SCRANTON CITY	30 60	81 60
OVERTIME	12 98	11 56	150 04	150 04	✓401K 100%	18 00	48 00
					✓ UNION DUES	9 75	29 25
					✓ MEDICAL INS	22 50	67 50
					✓ CREDIT UNION	30 00	90 00

pension

STATEMENT OF EARNINGS AND DEDUCTIONS   DETACH AND RETAIN FOR YOUR RECORDS

	EARNINGS	TAXES	DEDUCTIONS	NET PAY		PAY PERIOD	CHECK NUMBER	AMOUNT OF CHECK
CURRENT	900 00	– 194 00	– 80 25	= 625 75	BEGIN	02 / 01 / 93	200005413	625 75
YEAR TO DATE	2399 91	– 492 02	– 234 75	= 1673 14	END	02 / 15 / 93		

THE BACK OF THIS CHECK CONTAINS A GENERAL HOSPITAL CORP. FACSIMILE WATERMARK • CAN BE SEEN AT AN ANGLE

GH GENERAL HOSPITAL

Bank of
Pennsylvania
Philadelphia, PA

No. 200005413

PAY TO THE ORDER OF   ADAM WATERS   DATE   02 / 15 / 93

SIX HUNDRED TWENTY FIVE DOLLARS AND SEVENTY FIVE CENTS

2700 20 526   111-22-3333
ADAM WATERS
#1 WEST STREET
SCRANTON, PA   00000

PAY THIS AMOUNT
* * * * 625 75

NOT GOOD AFTER 60 DAYS FROM DATE ISSUED

MUST BE COUNTERSIGNED OVER $5000.00

⑆200005413⑆ ⑈053107989⑇ 480026251⑈

Routing #   Account #

Your Tax Deductions

Everyone who earns money pays taxes. Your tax money helps the government pay for roads, bridges, schools, and many other services.

You pay **federal income taxes** on your salary. Many states also have their own state income taxes. Some cities have their own city income taxes. You pay taxes for the city and state where you live.

You also pay **Social Security** and **Medicare taxes.** These taxes are listed on your paycheck stub as FICA/Medicare. FICA stands for Federal Insurance Contribution Act. It is Social Security tax. FICA

Federal income tax is the tax money you pay to the United States government on money you earn.

Social Security tax is money used by the government to send a monthly check to older adults.

money is used to pay older adults a monthly income. Medicare taxes pay for health insurance for older adults.

Your employer takes tax money out of your gross salary. When you start a new job, you will complete a W-4 form. This form tells your employer how much federal income tax you want to be taken out of your salary. The Necessary Skills Workshop on page 85 shows a W-4 form.

In January your employer will give you a form called a W-2. The W-2 form will show your gross salary for the year. It will show all the federal, state, and city income taxes that you paid. It will also show the amount of Social Security taxes you paid for the year.

1 Control number	6		
	Statutory employee ☐ Deceased ☐ Pension plan ☐ Legal rep. ☐ 942 emp. ☐ Subtotal ☐ Deferred compensation ☐ Void ☐	**Copy B To be filed with employee's FEDERAL Tax Return**	
2 Employer's name, address, and ZIP code			
		OMB No. 1545-0008	
		7 Allocated tips	9 Federal income tax withheld
3 Employer's identification number	4 Employer's state I.D. number	8 Advance EIC payment	10 Wages, tips, other compensation
5 Employee's social security number		11 Social security tax withheld	12 Social security wages
19 Employee's name, address and ZIP code		13 Social security tips	14 Medicare wages and tips
		15 Medicare tax withheld	16 Nonqualified plans
		17 See Instrs. for Box 17	18 Other
20	21	22 Dependent care benefits	23 Benefits included in Box 10
24 State income tax	25 State wages, tips, etc.	26 Name of state	27 Local income tax	28 Local wages, tips, etc.	29 Name of locality

C92-8 PT-1 • C92-6

Form W-2 Wage and Tax Statement 1992 (REV. 4-92)   I.R.S. APP.

This information is being furnished to the Internal Revenue Service   Department of the Treasury—Internal Revenue Service

Keep your W-2 form. You will need to mail a copy of your W-2 form to the **Internal Revenue Service**, or **IRS**, by April 15. You will have to file an income tax form with the IRS to report your salary and taxes each year. You may fill out a 1040, 1040A, or 1040EZ form. You can call the Internal Revenue Service to get help filling out your income tax form.

When you mail in your income tax form, the government will check to see that you paid the right amount of taxes. Sometimes workers pay too much. Then the government sends them a **refund.** Some workers do not pay enough taxes. Then the government sends them a bill to pay more taxes. When you fill out your income tax form, you will know if you owe the government more tax money. It is best to mail a check with your income tax form. That way you will not have to pay extra for being late.

Other Paycheck Deductions

Taxes are a deduction for all workers. You may want to have other deductions taken out of your paycheck. Every deduction you choose will lower the amount of money in your paycheck. You will have less money to spend.

What are some deductions you may want? You may want a health insurance plan. Some money will be taken out of each check to pay for insurance. You may want to join a labor union. Union dues will be taken out of your paycheck. You may choose to have a retirement plan. Then some money will be taken out of your salary for your retirement.

Your company may have a **credit union.** You may want to have a savings account in the credit union. Then money for a savings account with the credit union will be taken out of your paycheck.

As a new worker, think about the deductions you really need. You may need health insurance. But you may not need to join a credit union. The more deductions you have, the less money you take home.

Other Job Benefits

As a worker you will get a salary. You may also get other job benefits. These benefits can be worth thousands of dollars.

What are some job benefits that may be important to you?

1. You may get paid sick days. This benefit allows you to be absent a certain number of days each year. You will get paid for those days even though you are not at work.

2. You may get paid vacation days. This means you may be allowed to take off for one or two weeks. You will be paid for the weeks you are off.

3. You may get a group health insurance plan. This benefit will let you pay a low price for health insurance. Without this benefit you may have to pay much more for a good health insurance plan.

4. You may get a retirement plan. Many employers will add company money to your retirement plan. Then you will have an income after you retire.

It is important to understand your salary and your paycheck stub. Your net pay will always be less than your gross salary. Study your pay stub to understand all the deductions. You will always have money taken out for taxes. You will probably have other deductions, too. Learn which job benefits you can enjoy. Receiving a paycheck and job benefits are your rewards for being a part of the working world.

Completing a W-4 Form

Look at the sample W-4 form on page 85. It was filled out by Adam Waters. Adam has a wife and two children. His wife does not work full-time. Notice the following parts.

1 **Personal Allowances Worksheet.** This worksheet helps you figure out how many **allowances** you have. An allowance is the amount of money the government allows for the living expenses of a person. You do not pay taxes on that money. You may have allowances for your dependents. Dependents are the people you take care of, such as children and older adults. You may have an allowance for your spouse (husband or wife) who does not earn money. You may have an allowance if you are a single parent. You may have an allowance for day care.

2 **Employee's Withholding Allowance Certificate.** This part tells your employer how many allowances you are claiming. From this, the employer can tell how much federal income tax to withhold, or take out of your salary. Your employer sends that income tax to the Internal Revenue Service.

3 **Total Number of Allowances.** At the end of line 5, you write down the number of allowances you want to have. You may want to write down fewer allowances than you figured on the worksheet. If you take all the allowances you figured on your worksheet, you will take home more net pay each pay period. But then you may not have paid enough taxes by the end of the year. Then you will have to pay the government more tax money by April 15.

■ ■ ■

Use Adam's W-4 form to answer the following questions.

1. How many allowances is Adam taking for his children? _____

2. Is Adam taking an allowance for his wife? _____

3. Is Adam taking an allowance for day-care expenses? _____

4. What is Adam's social security number? _____

5. How many total allowances is Adam claiming? _____

1993 Form W-4

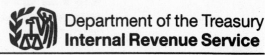

Department of the Treasury
Internal Revenue Service

Purpose. Complete Form W-4 so that your employer can withhold the correct amount of Federal income tax from your pay.

Exemption From Withholding. Read line 7 of the certificate below to see if you can claim exempt status. *If exempt, complete line 7; but do not complete lines 5 and 6.* No Federal income tax will be withheld from your pay. Your exemption is good for one year only. It expires February 15, 1994.

Basic Instructions. Employees who are not exempt should complete the Personal Allowances Worksheet. Additional worksheets are provided on page 2 for employees to adjust their withholding allowances based on itemized deductions, adjustments to income, or two-earner/two-job situations. Complete all worksheets that apply to your situation. The worksheets will help you figure the number of withholding allowances you are entitled to claim. However, you may claim fewer allowances than this.

Head of Household. Generally, you may claim head of household filing status on your tax return only if you are unmarried and pay more than 50% of the costs of keeping up a home for yourself and your dependent(s) or other qualifying individuals.

Nonwage Income. If you have a large amount of nonwage income, such as interest or dividends, you should consider making estimated tax payments using Form 1040-ES. Otherwise, you may find that you owe additional tax at the end of the year.

Two-Earner/Two-Jobs. If you have a working spouse or more than one job, figure the total number of allowances you are entitled to claim on all jobs using worksheets from only one Form W-4. This total should be divided among all jobs. Your withholding will usually be most accurate when all allowances are claimed on the W-4 filed for the highest paying job and zero allowances are claimed for the others.

Advance Earned Income Credit. If you are eligible for this credit, you can receive it added to your paycheck throughout the year. For details, get Form W-5 from your employer.

Check Your Withholding. After your W-4 takes effect, you can use **Pub. 919,** Is My Withholding Correct for 1993?, to see how the dollar amount you are having withheld compares to your estimated total annual tax. Call 1-800-829-3676 to order this publication. Check your local telephone directory for the IRS assistance number if you need further help.

Personal Allowances Worksheet

For 1993, the value of your personal exemption(s) is reduced if your income is over $108,450 ($162,700 if married filing jointly, $135,600 if head of household, or $81,350 if married filing separately). Get Pub. 919 for details.

A Enter "1" for **yourself** if no one else can claim you as a dependent . . . . **A** _1_

B Enter "1" if:
- You are single and have only one job; or
- You are married, have only one job, and your spouse does not work; or
- Your wages from a second job or your spouse's wages (or the total of both) are $1,000 or less.

. . **B** ____

C Enter "1" for your **spouse.** But, you may choose to enter -0- if you are married and have either a working spouse or more than one job (this may help you avoid having too little tax withheld) . . . . **C** _1_

D Enter number of **dependents** (other than your spouse or yourself) whom you will claim on your tax return . . . . . . **D** _2_

E Enter "1" if you will file as **head of household** on your tax return (see conditions under **Head of Household,** above) . . **E** ____

F Enter "1" if you have at least $1,500 of **child or dependent care expenses** for which you plan to claim a credit . . **F** ____

G Add lines A through F and enter total here. Note: *This amount may be different from the number of exemptions you claim on your return* ▶ **G** _4_

For accuracy, do all worksheets that apply.
- If you plan to **itemize or claim adjustments to income** and want to reduce your withholding, see the Deductions and Adjustments Worksheet on page 2.
- If you are **single** and have **more than one job** and your combined earnings from all jobs exceed $30,000 OR if you are **married** and have a **working spouse or more than one job,** and the combined earnings from all jobs exceed $50,000, see the Two-Earner/Two-Job Worksheet on page 2 if you want to avoid having too little tax withheld.
- If **neither** of the above situations applies, **stop here** and enter the number from line G on line 5 of Form W-4 below.

- - - - - - - - - - **Cut here and give the certificate to your employer. Keep the top portion for your records.** - - - - - - - - - -

Form W-4
Department of the Treasury
Internal Revenue Service

Employee's Withholding Allowance Certificate

▶ **For Privacy Act and Paperwork Reduction Act Notice, see reverse.**

OMB No. 1545-0010

1993

1 Type or print your first name and middle initial   Last name

Adam   L.   Waters

2 Your social security number

111-22-3333

Home address (number and street or rural route)

#1 West Street

3 ☐ Single ☒ Married ☐ Married, but withhold at higher Single rate.
Note: *If married, but legally separated, or spouse is a nonresident alien, check the Single box.*

City or town, state, and ZIP code

Scranton, Pennsylvania   00000

4 If your last name differs from that on your social security card, check here and call 1-800-772-1213 for more information . . . . ▶ ☐

5 Total number of allowances you are claiming (from line G above or from the worksheets on page 2 if they apply) . **5** _4_

6 Additional amount, if any, you want withheld from each paycheck . . . . **6** $ ____

7 I claim exemption from withholding for 1993 and I certify that I meet **ALL** of the following conditions for exemption:
- Last year I had a right to a refund of **ALL** Federal income tax withheld because I had **NO** tax liability; **AND**
- This year I expect a refund of **ALL** Federal income tax withheld because I expect to have **NO** tax liability; **AND**
- This year if my income exceeds $600 and includes nonwage income, another person cannot claim me as a dependent.
If you meet all of the above conditions, enter "EXEMPT" here . . . . ▶ **7**

Under penalties of perjury, I certify that I am entitled to the number of withholding allowances claimed on this certificate or entitled to claim exempt status.

Employee's signature ▶ *Adam Waters*   Date ▶ 2-1   , 19 93

8 Employer's name and address (Employer: Complete 8 and 10 only if sending to the IRS)

9 Office code (optional)

10 Employer identification number

Cat. No. 10220Q

WORKSHOP PRACTICE: Complete a W-4 Form

Whenever you start a new job, you fill out a W-4 form. Fill out the W-4 form on this page. Look back at Adam's W-4 form on page 85 for an example to follow.

Personal Allowances Worksheet   For 1993, the value of your personal exemption(s) is reduced if your income is over $108,450 ($162,700 if married filing jointly, $135,600 if head of household, or $81,350 if married filing separately). Get Pub. 919 for details.

A Enter "1" for **yourself** if no one else can claim you as a dependent . . . . **A** _____

B Enter "1" if: { • You are single and have only one job; or
• You are married, have only one job, and your spouse does not work; or
• Your wages from a second job or your spouse's wages (or the total of both) are $1,000 or less. } . . **B** _____

C Enter "1" for your **spouse.** But, you may choose to enter -0- if you are married and have either a working spouse or more than one job (this may help you avoid having too little tax withheld) . . . . **C** _____

D Enter number of **dependents** (other than your spouse or yourself) whom you will claim on your tax return . . . . . **D** _____

E Enter "1" if you will file as **head of household** on your tax return (see conditions under **Head of Household,** above) . **E** _____

F Enter "1" if you have at least $1,500 of **child or dependent care expenses** for which you plan to claim a credit . . **F** _____

G Add lines A through F and enter total here. **Note:** *This amount may be different from the number of exemptions you claim on your return* ▶ **G** _____

For accuracy, do all worksheets that apply. { • If you plan to **itemize or claim adjustments to income** and want to reduce your withholding, see the Deductions and Adjustments Worksheet on page 2.
• If you are **single** and have **more than one job** and your combined earnings from all jobs exceed $30,000 OR if you are **married** and have a **working spouse or more than one job,** and the combined earnings from all jobs exceed $50,000, see the Two-Earner/Two-Job Worksheet on page 2 if you want to avoid having too little tax withheld.
• If **neither** of the above situations applies, **stop here** and enter the number from line G on line 5 of Form W-4 below.

------------------ **Cut here and give the certificate to your employer. Keep the top portion for your records.** ------------------

Form **W-4** Department of the Treasury Internal Revenue Service	**Employee's Withholding Allowance Certificate** ▶ **For Privacy Act and Paperwork Reduction Act Notice, see reverse.**	OMB No. 1545-0010 19**93**

1 Type or print your first name and middle initial   Last name   **2** Your social security number

Home address (number and street or rural route)

3 ☐ Single ☐ Married ☐ Married, but withhold at higher Single rate.
Note: *If married, but legally separated, or spouse is a nonresident alien, check the Single box.*

City or town, state, and ZIP code

4 If your last name differs from that on your social security card, check here and call 1-800-772-1213 for more information . . . . ▶ ☐

5 Total number of allowances you are claiming (from line G above or from the worksheets on page 2 if they apply) . **5** _____

6 Additional amount, if any, you want withheld from each paycheck . . . . **6** $ _____

7 I claim exemption from withholding for 1993 and I certify that I meet **ALL** of the following conditions for exemption:
• Last year I had a right to a refund of **ALL** Federal income tax withheld because I had **NO** tax liability; **AND**
• This year I expect a refund of **ALL** Federal income tax withheld because I expect to have **NO** tax liability; **AND**
• This year if my income exceeds $600 and includes nonwage income, another person cannot claim me as a dependent.
If you meet all of the above conditions, enter "EXEMPT" here . . . . ▶ **7** _____

Under penalties of perjury, I certify that I am entitled to the number of withholding allowances claimed on this certificate or entitled to claim exempt status.

Employee's signature ▶   **Date** ▶   , 19

8 Employer's name and address (Employer: Complete 8 and 10 only if sending to the IRS)   **9** Office code (optional)   **10** Employer identification number

Cat. No. 10220Q

VOCABULARY: **Writing with Vocabulary Words**

Use six or more of the following words or phrases to write
a paragraph that tells about your paycheck and taxes.

gross salary
deductions
social security tax
refund
federal income tax
Medicare tax
net pay
Internal Revenue
    Service

_____

_____

_____

_____

_____

_____

_____

COMPREHENSION: **Write the Answer**

Write one or more sentences to answer each question.

1. Look at the diagram on page 79.
   a. What would the gross salary be for a pay period of one week? _____

   b. What would the gross salary be for a pay period of one month? _____

2. What is the difference between gross salary and net pay?

   _____

3. What is FICA/Medicare tax money used for?

   _____

4. What is a deduction that many workers have?

   _____

5. What is a benefit that a job may offer?

   _____

Thinking and Writing

Imagine that two employers want you to work for them.
They will both pay you the same salary. But the benefits are
different. Explain in your journal what kind of benefits you
want. Would benefits help you decide which job to take?

CHAPTER 9

HEALTH CARE

- How can you find a good doctor?
- What are the different kinds of health insurance you need?
- How does the government help pay for health care?

A **surgeon** is a doctor who can operate.

Health insurance helps you pay for different types of health care.

Lydia Rivera was nervous when she found a lump in her breast. She visited her doctor the next day. Her doctor sent her to a **surgeon.** The surgeon removed Lydia's lump in the hospital. Lydia was very happy when the surgeon told her that she did not have cancer. She was not as happy when she received the surgeon's bill. Lydia's **health insurance** paid most of the surgeon's bill. Health insurance helps you pay for the health care that you need.

Health insurance can help you pay medical bills.

You can take your child to a pediatrician or to a family practitioner.

Choosing Your Doctor

You need a doctor if you become sick. It is best to find a doctor when you are well. Then you will know who to call when you have a health problem.

There are many kinds of doctors. Usually **internists** treat only adults. **Family practitioners** treat children as well as adults. **Pediatricians** treat children. For illnesses that attack a certain part of the body, you may want to go to a **specialist.**

How can you find a good doctor? Sometimes friends will tell you about doctors they like. You can also call a nearby hospital. Ask the hospital to suggest a good doctor. Sometimes your insurance company will have a list of doctors. Choose one that is close to your home or your job. Make an appointment to meet the doctor. It is important to feel comfortable with your doctor.

Decide if you want a doctor who works alone or one who works with a small group of doctors. By choosing a doctor who works alone, you can see the same doctor all the time. By choosing a small group of doctors, you can use a few different doctors in the group. If one doctor is away on vacation, another doctor in the group will be there to care for you.

An **internist** is a doctor who treats diseases and problems found in adults.

A **family practitioner** is a doctor who is trained to treat both children and adults.

A **pediatrician** is a doctor who treats children.

A **specialist** is a doctor who has studied a special area of medicine and has passed special tests.

You may need to get health care at a clinic. At most clinics you pay only as much as you can afford. Sometimes a dentist, an eye doctor, and other specialists work together at the same clinic. To find a clinic, call the board of health or the health department in your city or town. Some hospitals have their own clinics.

Understanding Health Insurance

Health care is very expensive. A one-night stay in some hospitals is more than $500. Health insurance helps you pay for the care you need.

There are three kinds of health insurance.

1. **Hospitalization insurance** pays for a large part of the cost of staying in a hospital.

2. Medical insurance helps pay for doctor bills and medical tests.

3. **Major medical insurance** helps pay for very large health bills. It helps pay for **surgery** and expensive tests.

Health insurance helps you pay expensive bills. It would be hard to pay a $10,000 hospital bill or a $15,000 surgeon's bill. It is important to have hospitalization and major medical insurance to help you pay large bills. You need this protection if you or your family members become very sick.

Hospitalization insurance pays part of the cost of staying in a hospital.

Major medical insurance pays for very large medical bills, such as surgery.

Surgery is the use of medical tools to operate on the body.

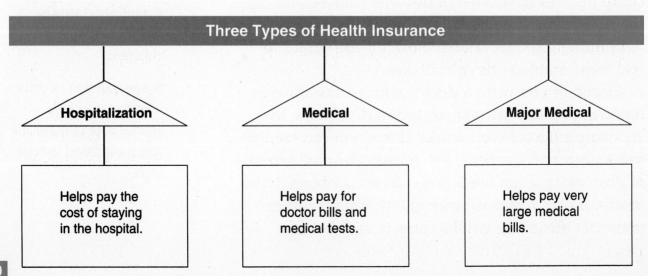

Three Types of Health Insurance

Hospitalization	Medical	Major Medical
Helps pay the cost of staying in the hospital.	Helps pay for doctor bills and medical tests.	Helps pay very large medical bills.

Many people buy group health insurance. Group plans cost less than private plans. Group plans may be provided through the company where you work. As long as you work for the company, you can have the group health insurance plan. If you leave your job, you may lose your group insurance.

Some people buy private health insurance plans. These plans are very expensive. Compare the price of a few plans from different insurance companies. Choose the plan that gives you the best protection and the best price.

Other Ways to Pay for Health Care

You may want to join a **Health Maintenance Organization,** or **HMO,** to pay less for your health care. You will pay a fee to be a member of the HMO. That fee allows you to get all the medical care you need for the year. The fee will pay for medical tests, doctor visits, surgery, and hospital stays. But you have to use HMO doctors and hospitals. If you go to a doctor or hospital that is not part of the HMO, you will have to pay the bills yourself.

The government also helps people pay for medical care. All people who are 65 years or older can receive **Medicare** insurance. Younger people with disabilities can sometimes receive Medicare. Medicare helps people pay for hospital stays and doctor bills. Sign up for Medicare at a social security office near your home.

Medicaid is another government health insurance program. It is for people with low incomes. Medicaid pays for hospital costs, medicine, tests, and doctor bills. Call the health and welfare office near your home to apply for Medicaid.

Every person needs health insurance. If you have health insurance now, find out more about it. Learn what it will and will not cover. If you do not have insurance, try to buy some kind of health plan that you can afford. You need an insurance plan that will pay for good health care when you need it.

A **Health Maintenance Organization (HMO)** is a group of doctors and hospitals that have agreed to provide medical services at a special rate to their members.

Medicare is a government health insurance program that pays for hospital stays for people who are at least 65 years old. Some disabled people can get Medicare.

Medicaid is a government health insurance program to provide health care for people with low incomes.

Completing a Health Insurance Form

Each time you see a doctor, you will complete a health insurance form. When you mail it to your health insurance company, the company will pay you back for part of your bill. Some doctors will send in the form for you. Then the insurance company will pay your bill by sending a check to your doctor.

Lydia Rivera took her son to the doctor. She completed the health insurance form on page 93. Notice the following parts.

1 **Employee and Dependent Information.** The first name to list is the owner of the insurance plan. A **dependent** is a person whose living expenses are paid by an adult. A child is the dependent of the parents. If the doctor visit is for a dependent, fill out that part. If the owner of the insurance is also the patient, then the dependent part would be left blank. Fill in employment information for other family members.

2 **Accident Information.** Complete this part if the patient had an accident. Insurance plans almost always pay for the total medical costs of accidents.

3 **Other Coverage Information.** Perhaps another family member has group health insurance with another job. Your insurance company will pay part of the bill. The other company will pay the rest.

4 **Itemized Bills.** Your doctor may give you a bill or bills listing all the expenses of your visit. Those bills need to be sent in with this form.

███

Use Lydia's insurance form to answer the following questions.

1. Who is Lydia's dependent? _____

2. Where does Lydia's husband work? _____

3. Why did Jesse visit the doctor? _____

4. What other health insurance company covers Lydia's family?

_____

AMERICAN
health insurance

Statement of Claim for
Medical Expense Benefits

Employee's Statement

Answer all questions below.
Omitted information will cause delays.

1

Name (print) First Middle Last	Social Security Number	Date of Birth	☐ Male
Lydia M. Rivera	092/36/7653	2/21/60	☑ Female

Present Address: Street   City   State Zip Code
609 East 7th Ave. Chicago IL 60629

Marital ☐ Single   ☐ Widowed
Status: ☑ Married ☐ Divorced

Telephone No.
(312) 555-4411
Area Code

Dependent Information — Complete this section only if expenses were incurred by an eligible dependent or dependents.

Name (print) First Middle Last	Social Security Number	If dependent (other than spouse) is over
Jesse C. Rivera	122/78/1529	age 18 answer the following:

Date of Birth	Relationship			Marital ☑ Single	☐ Disabled
11/14/89	Son	☑ Male ☐ Female		Status: ☐ Married	☐ Student: No. of Units_____

Family Employment — Complete this section only if other members, including dependent minors, are employed.

Name of Family Member (print) First Middle Last	Relationship	Date of Birth	Employer's Telephone No.
Carlos R. Rivera	husband	7/14/59	(312) 555-1100 Area Code

Employer's Name (print)
Central Animal Hospital

Employer's Address — Street   City   State   Zip Code
40 Orchard St.   Chicago   IL 60609

2

Accident Information — Complete this section only if claim is result of accidental injury or occupational sickness.

Date of Accident	Time of Accident		Where Did the Accident Occur? (City, State)	Did the Accident/Sickness
2/2/94	7:00	☐ A.M. ☑ P.M.	609 East 7th Ave, Chicago, IL	Happen at Work? ☐ Yes ☑ No

Describe Accident or Occupational Sickness
Jesse slipped on a wet floor and turned his ankle.

Medicare Information — Complete this section only if Patient is eligible for Medicare.

Please Attach a Copy of the "Explanation of Benefits" Statement From Your Medicare Insurance Carrier.	Medicare	Part A	Effective Date	Part B	Effective Date

3

Other Coverage Information — This section must always be completed.

Are any benefits or services provided under another group insurance plan or any prepayment plan, or pursuant to any law (Federal, State, or Local) on account of the treatment reported on this claim?
☑ Yes   ☐ No
If "Yes," answer (A) or (B), whichever applies, and (C).

A. Other Insurance Coverage is: ☑ Group ☐ Individual
☐ Other (specify) ➤ All American Insurance

B. Name or Type of Law is (e.g., Medicaid, Champus, No-Fault)

C. Give Name and Address of Other Company or Organization Providing Benefits or Services.
Name All American Insurance
Address 999 W. Broadway
City Chicago   State IL   Zip Code 60613

Please Indicate Plan Identification No. or Group No.(s). ➤ 7836576

4

Itemized Bills — Attach itemized bills for expenses not reported on this form. All such miscellaneous bills must show:

a. Employee's Name   b. Patient's Name (if not employee)   c. Name and Address of Provider of Services   d. Diagnosis

e. Complete Description of Services Rendered   f. Initials of Attending or Prescribing Physician   g. Dates (month, day, year) of Service

Certifications and Medical Authorization

I authorize any insurance company, organization, employer, hospital, physician, or pharmacist to release any information requested with regard to this claim and the expenses reported.
I certify that the information I furnish in support of this claim is true and correct. I know it is a crime to fill out this form with facts I know are false or to leave out facts I know are important.

Signed (Employee)
Lydia M. Rivera Date 2/2/94
Signed (Dependent patient, not minor)

Date

Payment of Benefits

I hereby authorize payment of benefits otherwise payable to me up to the stated charges to the provider(s) of services for all bills included with this statement — unless otherwise noted.

I understand I am financially responsible for any amounts not payable or not covered by the plan.

Signed (Employee)

Lydia M. Rivera Date 2/2/94

CHECK YOUR SKILLS

WORKSHOP PRACTICE: **Complete a Health Insurance Form**

Practice filling out a health insurance form. Complete the sections below. Keep this page. Use it as a guide whenever you need to complete a health insurance claim. Use the Necessary Skills Workshop on pages 92–93 to help you complete this form.

Statement of Claim for
Medical Expense Benefits

Employee's Statement	**Answer all questions below.** **Omitted information will cause delays.**

Name (print) First Middle Last	Social Security Number / /	Date of Birth	☐ Male ☐ Female

Present Address: Street City State Zip Code	Marital ☐ Single ☐ Widowed Status: ☐ Married ☐ Divorced	Telephone No. ( ) Area Code

Family Employment — Complete this section only if other members, including dependent minors, are employed.

Name of Family Member (print) First Middle Last	Relationship	Date of Birth	Employer's Telephone No. ( ) Area Code
Employer's Name (print)	Employer's Address — Street City State Zip Code		

Other Coverage Information — This section must always be completed.

Are any benefits or services provided under another group insurance plan or any prepayment plan, or pursuant to any law (Federal, State, or Local) on account of the treatment reported on this claim? ☐ Yes ☐ No If "Yes," answer (A) or (B), whichever applies, and (C).	C. Give Name and Address of Other Company or Organization Providing Benefits or Services. Name Address
A. Other Insurance Coverage is: ☐ Group ☐ Individual ☐ Other (specify) ➤	City State Zip Code
B. Name or Type of Law is (e.g., Medicaid, Champus, No-Fault)	Please Indicate Plan Identification No. or Group No.(s). ➤

COMPREHENSION: **Write the Answer**

Write one or more sentences to answer each question.

1. How can you find a good doctor?

_____

_____

_____

2. What three kinds of health insurance do people need?

_____

_____

_____

3. Why do many people buy group health insurance instead of private health insurance?

_____

_____

4. Why do many people join an HMO?

_____

_____

5. What is the difference between Medicare and Medicaid?

_____

_____

VOCABULARY: Finish the Sentence

Choose one of the following words or phrases to complete each sentence. Write the word or phrase on the correct line.

hospitalization
specialist
surgeon
family practitioner
major medical

1. A _____ is a doctor who treats children and adults.

2. A _____ is a doctor who has studied a special area of medicine, such as skin diseases.

3. _____ is insurance that pays part of the cost of staying in the hospital.

4. _____ is insurance that pays for very large medical bills.

5. A _____ is a doctor who can operate.

Thinking and Writing

Think about the kind of health insurance you own. Is it enough protection for you? In your journal explain what your health insurance covers. Tell what you can do to improve your health insurance.

CHAPTER 10

SOCIAL SECURITY

THINK ABOUT AS YOU READ

- What are five Social Security programs?
- Why do some people get survivors benefits?
- How are SSI benefits different from other Social Security programs?

Survivors benefits are monthly checks that are paid to certain family members of a worker who has died.

Social Security is a federal program that provides monthly income to many people.

Lauren Brown had three children when her husband was killed in an accident. Lauren had a good job, but she depended on her husband's income. She worried about how she would care for her family without his income. Lauren learned that she could get **survivors benefits** from a federal plan called **Social Security.** The Social Security money Lauren receives each month helps her care for her family. In this chapter you will learn how Social Security works and how it may help you.

Social Security helps families like Lauren's.

How Social Security Works

You become part of the Social Security plan when you get a Social Security card. Your card has your Social Security number. Most parents get Social Security cards for their children soon after they are born. If you were born in a different country, you have to fill out a special Social Security form to get a card.

The amount of Social Security money workers can get is based on both the number of years they have worked and their income. You receive Social Security **credits** for each year that you work. You can earn as many as four credits in one year. To receive the most benefits, you have to earn 40 credits. Most people earn these 40 credits by working for ten years. If you have fewer than 40 credits, you will receive fewer benefits.

All Social Security programs are paid for with tax money. Most workers have to pay Social Security taxes, or FICA, to the Internal Revenue Service. Check your paystub to see how much of your income is used to pay the FICA tax.

Workers who earn higher incomes usually receive larger Social Security benefits. Workers who earn less money usually get lower benefits. For most people, Social Security does not provide enough money to pay for all of their needs.

The Social Security agency has a record of your credits and your income. Have your Social Security records checked once in three years. Be sure that your records have the correct information about the number of credits and the amount of money you have earned. If there are mistakes on your records, you may receive lower benefits than you deserve. To check your records, call or visit a Social Security office near your home. A Social Security worker will help you get the information you need. Social Security never charges you for information or services.

To receive Social Security benefits, you earn **credits** for the time you spend working.

Retirement is the period when an older person no longer works.

A spouse is a husband or wife.

Supplemental Security Income (SSI) pays monthly checks to low-income people who are 65 or disabled.

How Social Security Helps People

Social Security has offices in every state. People in every state receive the same Social Security benefits. There are five Social Security programs.

1. **Retirement** benefits are paid to older people.

2. Medicare is a health insurance program. It is for people 65 or older and for many people with disabilities.

3. Survivors benefits are paid to certain family members if a parent or **spouse** dies.

4. Disability benefits are paid to workers who are disabled and sometimes to their family members.

5. **Supplemental Security Income**, or **SSI**, benefits are paid to some people with low incomes.

Social Security Programs

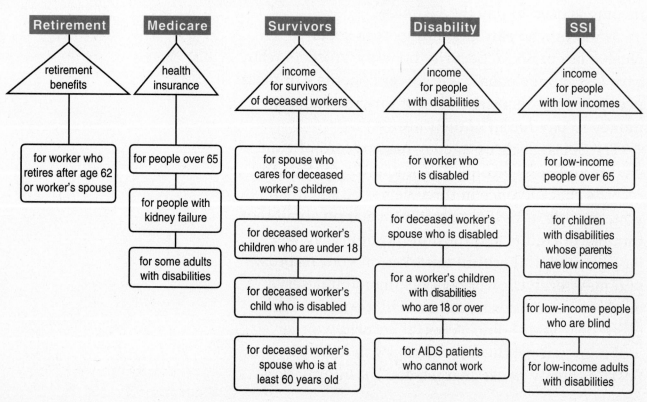

Retirement — retirement benefits
- for worker who retires after age 62 or worker's spouse

Medicare — health insurance
- for people over 65
- for people with kidney failure
- for some adults with disabilities

Survivors — income for survivors of deceased workers
- for spouse who cares for deceased worker's children
- for deceased worker's children who are under 18
- for deceased worker's child who is disabled
- for deceased worker's spouse who is at least 60 years old

Disability — income for people with disabilities
- for worker who is disabled
- for deceased worker's spouse who is disabled
- for a worker's children with disabilities who are 18 or over
- for AIDS patients who cannot work

SSI — income for people with low incomes
- for low-income people over 65
- for children with disabilities whose parents have low incomes
- for low-income people who are blind
- for low-income adults with disabilities

Retirement and Medicare

Most people look forward to getting Social Security retirement benefits. You can receive benefits if you have worked and earned 40 credits. You also have to be old enough to receive retirement benefits. If you were born after 1960, you can receive full benefits after you are 67 years old. If you were born before 1960, call Social Security to learn when you can receive full retirement benefits. You can start to collect benefits at age 62, but you will get less money each month for the rest of your life. A husband or wife who has never worked can collect benefits if the spouse has earned enough work credits.

Most people can get Medicare benefits if they are 65 years old. People of any age who have **kidney failure** can get Medicare. You can also get Medicare benefits if you have received Social Security disability benefits for 24 months. Medicare helps pay hospital bills. People can buy more Medicare insurance to help pay their doctor bills.

When a person's kidneys stop working, this sickness is called **kidney failure.** Kidneys help remove wastes from the blood.

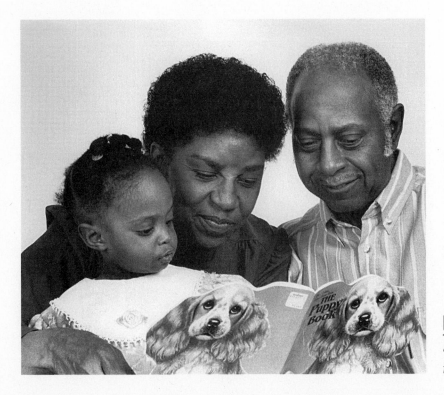

Social Security helps people enjoy their retirement.

Survivors Benefits

Survivors benefits are paid to certain family members of a **deceased** worker. The deceased worker had to pay Social Security taxes and earn at least six credits in order for the family to get survivors benefits. There are four groups of people who can get survivors benefits.

1. The spouse who takes care of the deceased worker's children can get benefits. Those children have to be disabled or under age 16.

2. The deceased worker's children can get benefits. The children have to be under 18. They can be under 19 if they are full-time students. They cannot be married.

3. A deceased worker's child who is disabled will get benefits until that child marries. The child's disability must have started before age 22.

4. A spouse can get survivors benefits starting at age 60.

A **deceased** person has died.

Social Security programs help people with disabilities.

Disability and SSI Benefits

Disability benefits are paid to people with **severe** disabilities. The Social Security agency decides whether the disability is severe. People with disabilities who work at good jobs and earn good salaries cannot get disability benefits. There are four groups of people who may get disability benefits.

1. Workers who become disabled after they have earned enough credits may get benefits.

2. A deceased worker's spouse who is disabled may get benefits.

3. Children with disabilities who are over age 18 may get benefits if one of their parents has enough credits.

4. People who cannot work because they have AIDS or **HIV infection** may get benefits.

You can apply for benefits as soon as you become disabled. If you can receive disability benefits, your payments will begin after six months. You can get benefits until you are able to return to work. Some people receive benefits for many years.

SSI benefits are paid to help people with low incomes. People who are blind, disabled, or over age 65 can get SSI benefits. Low-income parents with children who are disabled can also get benefits. SSI is different from other Social Security programs. You do not have to work and earn credits to get benefits. Instead, you have to show that you have a low income.

Millions of Americans receive money from Social Security each month. During your working years, you pay taxes to this plan. One day you will be able to enjoy the benefits of Social Security.

Severe means very bad or serious. A severe disability is a disability that prevents a person from earning a good salary.

A person with **HIV infection** has the virus that causes AIDS.

Replacing a Lost Social Security Card

The form on page 103 is a sample of the form used to apply for a Social Security card. You can get a real form from the Social Security office. You use the same form if you lose your card and need another one. You also complete the same form if you have changed your name. A change in name can be from a marriage, divorce, or court order.

To replace a Social Security card, you have to show at least one piece of identification that proves who you are. Some forms of identification are a driver's license, school record, hospital record, or a passport. The identification papers will be returned to you. Take or mail your completed form with identification to your nearest Social Security office.

Lauren Brown lost her Social Security card. She completed the application to replace her card. She used her health insurance card for identification. She knew her Social Security number. You keep the same number for life. It is a good idea to memorize your number. Even though you know your Social Security number, you may need to show your card when you get a new job. Study the form on page 103. Notice that on the form, you do not have to complete section 5.

■■■

Answer the following questions about Lauren's application.

1. Is it acceptable to use a pencil to fill out this form? _____

2. What was Lauren's name at birth? _____

3. Is it acceptable to abbreviate on this form? _____

4. What is Lauren's mother's maiden name? _____

5. What is Lauren's father's name? _____

6. What was the name Lauren used on her last Social Security card?

_____

SOCIAL SECURITY ADMINISTRATION
Application for a Social Security Card

INSTRUCTIONS

- Print or type using black or blue ink. DO NOT USE PENCIL.
- After you complete this form, take or mail it along with the required documents to your nearest Social Security office.
- If you are completing this form for someone else, answer the questions as they apply to that person. Then, sign your name in question 16.

1 NAME To Be Shown On Card

▶ Lauren   Jessica   Brown
FIRST   FULL MIDDLE NAME   LAST

FULL NAME AT BIRTH IF OTHER THAN ABOVE

Lauren   Jessica   Johnson
FIRST   FULL MIDDLE NAME   LAST

OTHER NAMES USED

2 MAILING ADDRESS Do Not Abbreviate

▶ 135 Pearl Street   Apartment 2H
STREET ADDRESS, APT. NO., PO BOX, RURAL ROUTE NO.

Jersey City   New Jersey   07304
CITY   STATE   ZIP CODE

3 CITIZENSHIP (Check One)

☑ U.S. Citizen ☐ Legal Alien Allowed To Work ☐ Legal Alien Not Allowed To Work ☐ Foreign Student Allowed Restricted Employment ☐ Conditionally Legalized Alien Allowed To Work ☐ Other (See Instructions On Page 2)

4 SEX

☐ Male ☑ Female

5 RACE/ETHNIC DESCRIPTION (Check One Only – Voluntary)

☐ Asian, Asian-American Or Pacific Islander ☐ Hispanic ☑ Black (Not Hispanic) ☐ North American Indian Or Alaskan Native ☐ White (Not Hispanic)

6 DATE OF BIRTH   8/24/63
MONTH DAY YEAR

7 PLACE OF BIRTH (Do Not Abbreviate)   Trenton   New Jersey
CITY   STATE OR FOREIGN COUNTRY

8 MOTHER'S MAIDEN NAME

Donna   Mary   Mason
FIRST   FULL MIDDLE NAME   LAST NAME AT HER BIRTH

9 FATHER'S NAME

Henry   Paul   Johnson
FIRST   FULL MIDDLE NAME   LAST

10 Has the person in item 1 ever received a Social Security number before?

☑ Yes (If "yes," answer questions 11-13.)   ☐ No (If "no," go on to question 14.)   ☐ Don't Know (If "don't know," go on to question 14.)

11 Enter the Social Security number previously assigned to the person listed in item 1.

8 8 8 – 9 9 – 7 7 7 7

12 Enter the name shown on the most recent Social Security card issued for the person listed in item 1.

Lauren   Jessica   Brown
FIRST   MIDDLE   LAST

13 Enter any different date of birth if used on an earlier application for a card.
MONTH DAY YEAR

14 TODAY'S DATE ▶ 3/1/94
MONTH DAY YEAR

15 DAYTIME PHONE NUMBER ▶ (609) 555-1212
AREA CODE

Deliberately furnishing (or causing to be furnished) false information on this application is a crime punishable by fine or imprisonment, or both.

16 YOUR SIGNATURE

▶ Lauren Jessica Brown

17 YOUR RELATIONSHIP TO THE PERSON IN ITEM 1 IS:

☑ Self ☐ Natural or Adoptive Parent ☐ Legal Guardian ☐ Other (Specify)

WORKSHOP PRACTICE: Applying for a Social Security Card

Complete a sample application for a Social Security card for yourself or a family member. You can look back at Lauren's completed form in the Necessary Skills Workshop on page 103.

SOCIAL SECURITY ADMINISTRATION
Application for a Social Security Card

1 NAME
To Be Shown On Card

FIRST	FULL MIDDLE NAME	LAST

FULL NAME AT BIRTH IF OTHER THAN ABOVE

FIRST	FULL MIDDLE NAME	LAST

OTHER NAMES USED

2 MAILING ADDRESS
Do Not Abbreviate

STREET ADDRESS, APT. NO., PO BOX, RURAL ROUTE NO.

CITY	STATE	ZIP CODE

3 CITIZENSHIP
(Check One)

☐ U.S. Citizen ☐ Legal Alien Allowed To Work ☐ Legal Alien Not Allowed To Work ☐ Foreign Student Allowed Restricted Employment ☐ Conditionally Legalized Alien Allowed To Work ☐ Other (See Instructions On Page 2)

4 SEX

☐ Male ☐ Female

5 RACE/ETHNIC DESCRIPTION
(Check One Only – Voluntary)

☐ Asian, Asian-American Or Pacific Islander ☐ Hispanic ☐ Black (Not Hispanic) ☐ North American Indian Or Alaskan Native ☐ White (Not Hispanic)

6 DATE OF BIRTH

MONTH DAY YEAR

7 PLACE OF BIRTH
(Do Not Abbreviate)

CITY STATE OR FOREIGN COUNTRY

8 MOTHER'S MAIDEN NAME

FIRST	FULL MIDDLE NAME	LAST NAME AT HER BIRTH

9 FATHER'S NAME

FIRST	FULL MIDDLE NAME	LAST

10 Has the person in item 1 ever received a Social Security number before?

☐ Yes (If "yes," answer questions 11-13.) ☐ No (If "no," go on to question 14.) ☐ Don't Know (If "don't know," go on to question 14.)

11 Enter the Social Security number previously assigned to the person listed in item 1.

☐☐☐ – ☐☐ – ☐☐☐☐

12 Enter the name shown on the most recent Social Security card issued for the person listed in item 1.

FIRST	MIDDLE	LAST

13 Enter any different date of birth if used on an earlier application for a card. _____

MONTH DAY YEAR

14 TODAY'S DATE ▶ _____
MONTH DAY YEAR

15 DAYTIME PHONE NUMBER ▶ ( )
AREA CODE

Deliberately furnishing (or causing to be furnished) false information on this application is a crime punishable by fine or imprisonment, or both.

16 YOUR SIGNATURE
▶ _____

17 YOUR RELATIONSHIP TO THE PERSON IN ITEM 1 IS:
☐ Self ☐ Natural or Adoptive Parent ☐ Legal Guardian ☐ Other (Specify)

VOCABULARY: Writing with Vocabulary Words

Use five or more of the following words or phrases to write a paragraph that tells about the Social Security system.

Social Security
retirement
survivors benefits
Medicare
disability
deceased
credits

_____

_____

_____

_____

_____

_____

_____

COMPREHENSION: Write the Answer

Write one or more sentences to answer each question.

1. Where does the government get money to pay Social Security benefits?

_____

2. How many credits does a person need to have in order to receive the most Social Security benefits? _____

_____

3. Who can get Social Security disability benefits? _____

_____

4. Who can get Social Security survivors benefits? _____

_____

5. Who can get Supplemental Security Income? _____

_____

Thinking and Writing

Do you think it is fair that workers who earn higher incomes will receive more Social Security benefits than workers who earn less money? In your journal explain why you think this system is fair or unfair.

DISCRIMINATION

Discrimination means treating people unfairly because of age, sex, race, religion, or disability.

Carmen Sanchez is deaf. She knows how to speak, but some people find it hard to understand her. Carmen worked as a typist for a few years. Then she tried to get a better-paying job as a typist for a different business. The employer did not hire Carmen. A different person who could not type as fast was hired instead. Carmen felt she did not get the job because of **discrimination** against workers who are disabled.

All people have the right to be treated fairly.

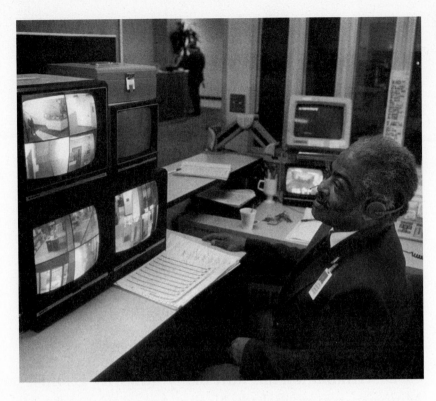

Workers cannot be forced to retire before age 70.

In this chapter you will read about discrimination. You will learn what you can do if someone **discriminates against** you.

Understanding Discrimination

Discrimination is the unfair treatment of people because they are different. People may be discriminated against because of their age, sex, or religion. They may be discriminated against because of their race or disability. Prejudiced people may discriminate against people who come to live in America from other countries.

Many people are hurt by job discrimination each year. This means you might not get hired because of your race, sex, age, religion, or disability. Another kind of job discrimination happens when you are paid less money for doing a job because of your age, race, or sex. Job discrimination also happens when you deserve a better job but you do not get it because of your sex, race, religion, or disability. Instead, the job is given to a person with less skill. Job discrimination is **illegal.**

To **discriminate against** someone means to treat that person unfairly.

Illegal means against the law.

Your **national origin** is the country where you were born.

Sexual harassment is acts and words about sex that make you feel uncomfortable on the job.

Minority groups are groups of people in a nation that are not like most people in that nation. For example, the difference may be race or religion.

People are also hurt by housing discrimination. This means you cannot buy or rent a home because of your race, religion, or **national origin.** Housing discrimination is also illegal.

Sexual harassment is another form of discrimination. Sexual harassment can be words or acts that make you feel uncomfortable on the job. Your employer may pressure you for a date. You may feel that you have to go on the date or you will not move up in the company. Both men and women employers can be guilty of sexual harassment. Sometimes sexual harassment is done by other workers in the company. Sexual harassment is illegal.

Who Has Suffered Most from Discrimination?

Discrimination has hurt many **minority groups.** Minority groups include Native Americans and Hispanics. African Americans and Asians have been discriminated against because of their race. Jews have faced discrimination because of their religion.

Women also face discrimination. They are sometimes paid less money than men for doing the same work. It is harder for women to become leaders in business and government.

People who are disabled face discrimination at work. Many employers do not want to hire them. They also face discrimination in public places. People who are blind cannot read the price labels in stores. People in wheelchairs have trouble finding stores, restaurants, hotels, and bathrooms where they can move around easily.

Laws That Fight Discrimination

The fourteenth amendment to the Constitution says the laws must give equal protection to all people. Because of this amendment, laws have been passed to fight discrimination.

Many stores and businesses are planning for the needs of people with disabilities.

The Civil Rights Act of 1964 was the first important law to fight discrimination. This law said that all people must be hired and fired fairly. It also said that all people have the right to use public places like restaurants, parks, and hotels.

Affirmative action programs were started because of the 1964 law. These programs help African Americans and other minority groups get better jobs. They also help people with disabilities. Many large companies now hire more women and more people from minority groups because of these programs.

Other laws have been passed to fight discrimination. Here are some ways these laws are working against discrimination.

1. Employers cannot discriminate when they hire and fire workers. They cannot discriminate when giving people better jobs.

2. Men and women must be paid the same money for doing the same work.

Affirmative action programs give a certain number of jobs to women, members of minority groups, and people with disabilities.

All students have the right to take part in classroom activities.

3. It is illegal to refuse to hire people because they are more than 40 years old. Workers cannot be forced to retire before the age of 70.

4. Labor unions cannot refuse to accept new members because of their age, race, sex, or disability.

5. All people have the right to live any place they can afford. It is illegal to refuse to sell or rent to a person from a minority group.

To **sue** means to take someone to court.

6. You have the right to **sue** people who discriminate against you.

7. Employers cannot discriminate against pregnant women. A woman cannot be forced to leave her job because she is pregnant.

Illegal aliens are people who come to the United States from other nations without the permission of the United States government.

8. Employers cannot refuse to hire people because of their national origin. But employers cannot hire **illegal aliens.**

9. Employers cannot refuse to hire people because of their religion. Workers cannot be forced to do activities that are against their religion.

10. Employers cannot refuse to hire people with disabilities who have the skills to do the job. Businesses have to try to make changes in their buildings to make it easier for people with disabilities to work there.

11. Every child who is disabled has the right to a public school education.

Discrimination laws do not protect workers who use illegal drugs. Employers can test their workers for drug abuse. They do not have to hire people who use illegal drugs. They can fire workers for using illegal drugs.

Carrying Out Laws Against Discrimination

Laws protect you from discrimination. Agencies carry out these laws. The **Equal Employment Opportunity Commission,** or **EEOC,** makes sure that laws against job discrimination are obeyed. This federal agency has offices in many states.

The EEOC can help you if you have suffered from job discrimination. Call the EEOC if you feel an employer discriminated against you. An EEOC worker will talk to you about your problem. You will be asked to fill out a form. Then EEOC workers will try to learn more about what happened. Employers can be punished if the EEOC proves that they have not obeyed discrimination laws.

Other agencies protect your right to fair housing. Perhaps you faced discrimination when buying or renting a home. Call the Human Rights Commission in your area. This agency will protect your housing rights.

Many laws have been passed that protect you from discrimination. You have the right to be treated fairly when you look for a home or a job. Government agencies can help you keep these important rights.

The **Equal Employment Opportunity Commission (EEOC)** is a federal agency that makes sure that laws against job discrimination are obeyed.

Filing a Discrimination Charge

If you have faced job discrimination, the EEOC can help you. Call the EEOC office nearest your home. An EEOC worker will ask you to explain how your employer discriminated against you. If the EEOC worker agrees that there was a problem, you will be sent a discrimination charge form. After the EEOC receives your completed form, workers there will check your story. An employer can be punished if the EEOC finds that the employer discriminated against you.

Carmen Sanchez felt that she was discriminated against because she is deaf. Notice the following parts of Carmen's discrimination form.

1 **State or Local Agency.** If you are discriminated against at your job, report to the employment office at your job first. If no one helps you fill out this form, then call your state or local human rights office. If a company does not hire you because of discrimination, call your state human rights office or the EEOC office nearest you.

2 **Who Discriminated Against You.** You may list more than one person, group, or company that discriminated against you.

3 **Cause of Discrimination.** "Retaliation" means someone is trying to get even with you, perhaps for reporting illegal acts at your job. "Other" may include sexual harassment.

■ ■ ■

Answer these questions about Carmen's completed form.

1. Which employer is this charge against? _____

2. What kind of job did Carmen want? _____

3. How fast can Carmen type? _____

4. How fast can the person who was hired type? _____

5. Why does Carmen feel that she has been discriminated against?

_____

CHARGE OF DISCRIMINATION

This form is affected by the Privacy Act of 1974; see Privacy Act Statement on reverse before completing this form.

ENTER CHARGE NUMBER
☐ FEPA
☐ EEOC

1   State of Illinois Human Rights Commission _____ and EEOC
(State or Local Agency, if any)

NAME *(Indicate Mr., (Ms.) or Mrs.)*
Carmen Sanchez

HOME TELEPHONE NO. *(Include Area Code)*
312-555-1907

STREET ADDRESS   CITY, STATE AND ZIP CODE
124 Montrose Avenue West Chicago, IL 60613

COUNTY
Cook

2   NAMED IS THE EMPLOYER, LABOR ORGANIZATION, EMPLOYMENT AGENCY, APPRENTICESHIP COMMITTEE, STATE OR LOCAL GOVERNMENT AGENCY WHO DISCRIMINATED AGAINST ME *(If more than one, list below.)*

NAME Smith's Box Company	NO. OF EMPLOYEES/MEMBERS 35	TELEPHONE NUMBER *(Include Area Code)* 312-555-6302

STREET ADDRESS
25 Birch Avenue South

CITY, STATE AND ZIP CODE
Chicago, IL 60617

NAME

TELEPHONE NUMBER *(Include Area Code)*

STREET ADDRESS

CITY, STATE AND ZIP CODE

3   CAUSE OF DISCRIMINATION BASED ON *(Check appropriate box(es))*

☐ RACE ☐ COLOR ☐ SEX ☐ RELIGION ☐ NATIONAL ORIGIN
☐ AGE ☐ RETALIATION ☑ OTHER *(Specify)* disability

DATE MOST RECENT OR CONTINUING DISCRIMINATION TOOK PLACE *(Month, day, year)*
Jan. 10, 1994

THE PARTICULARS ARE *(If additional space is needed, attach extra sheet(s)):*

I applied for a typing job at Smith's Box Company. I can type 65 words a minute, and I had a good job recommendation from my last typing job. Mr. Smith told me I could not have the job because he needed a better typist. Then I learned from a friend who works for Mr. Smith that he hired a different typist who types only 50 words a minute. I feel I didn't get the job because Mr. Smith did not want a deaf typist. He hired a hearing person who does not type as well as I do.

☑ I also want this charge filed with the EEOC. I will advise the agencies if I change my address or telephone number and I will cooperate fully with them in the processing of my charge in accordance with their procedures.

NOTARY - (When necessary to meet State and Local Requirements)

I swear or affirm that I have read the above charge and that it is true to the best of my knowledge, information and belief.

I declare under penalty of perjury that the foregoing is true and correct.

SIGNATURE OF COMPLAINANT

SUBSCRIBED AND SWORN TO BEFORE ME THIS DATE
(Day, month, and year)

Feb. 11, 1994
Date

Carmen Sanchez
Charging Party *(Signature)*

WORKSHOP PRACTICE: File a Discrimination Charge

Read this paragraph about discrimination.

Janet Wilson worked at the All Star Company for one year. She was the company's only woman worker. She always finished all of her work each day. On February 7, her employer fired her for being a slow worker. The employer hired a male worker for the job. Janet felt that she was fired for unfair reasons. She decided to file a Charge of Discrimination with the EEOC.

Imagine that you are Janet Wilson. Complete this part of the discrimination charge form. Use it to explain why you felt you were discriminated against.

CHARGE OF DISCRIMINATION

CAUSE OF DISCRIMINATION BASED ON *(Check appropriate box(es))*	DATE MOST RECENT OR CONTINUING DISCRIMINATION TOOK PLACE *(Month, day, year)*
☐RACE ☐COLOR ☐SEX ☐RELIGION ☐NATIONAL ORIGIN ☐AGE ☐RETALIATION ☐OTHER *(Specify)*	

THE PARTICULARS ARE *(If additional space is needed, attach extra sheet(s)):*

VOCABULARY: Writing with Vocabulary Words

Use five or more of the following words or phrases to write a paragraph that tells about discrimination.

discrimination
employers
sue
EEOC
sexual harassment
minority groups
illegal

_____

_____

_____

_____

_____

_____

_____

COMPREHENSION: Finish the Paragraph

Use the following words or phrases to finish the paragraph. Write the words you choose on the correct lines.

Civil Rights Act
disability
housing
job
national origin
pregnant

People may face discrimination because of their age, race, sex, religion, _____ , or _____ . People may face _____ discrimination from employers. An employer cannot refuse to hire a _____ woman. People may face _____ discrimination when they want to buy or rent a home. The first important law to end discrimination was the _____ of 1964.

Thinking and Writing

Have you or someone you know been hurt by discrimination? If not, imagine that you have. In your journal explain what happened and what actions could be taken against this type of discrimination.

GLOSSARY

A

affirmative action programs Programs that give a certain number of jobs to women, members of minority groups, and people with disabilities. page 109

alcohol A chemical found in wine, beer, and liquor. It changes the way the brain thinks and works. page 62

allowance The amount of money the government allows for the basic needs of a person. You do not pay taxes on that money. page 84

application The form you fill out to apply for a job. page 18

apply To ask for a job and then prepare forms or letters to get the job. page 16

apprentice Someone who learns skills on the job. page 11

attitude The feelings and behavior you show about other people or ideas. page 72

B

benefit The money that an insurance company pays a worker. page 64

benefits The extra items a job offers, such as health insurance, paid vacation, and sick days. pages 34, 79

brief To be short in time or in length. page 46

C

car-pool A group of people who travel in one car so that they do not have to drive separate cars to the same place. page 53

civil service jobs Jobs with the government. page 18

classified ads Ads in the newspaper for jobs, houses, and apartments. page 17

commuter trains Trains that carry people from one city to another. page 53

compromise To reach an agreement by having each side give up some of its demands. page 71

confident Being sure of yourself and your skills. page 44

cooperative Working together with other people. page 71

co-workers People who work with you. page 61

credits Social Security points you earn for the time you spend working. page 97

credit union A place where members have savings accounts and get loans. page 82

criticism A statement that finds fault with something you do. page 73

criticized When other people find fault with you. page 73

D

deceased Dead. page 100

deductions The money taken out of your paycheck for taxes, health insurance, and other items. page 79

dependent A person whose living expenses are paid by an adult. page 92

disability A problem that makes a person less able to do certain things. page 31

discriminate against To treat a person unfairly. page 107

discrimination Treating people unfairly because of age, sex, race, religion, or disability. page 106

E

employees People who work for a company or business. page 66

employer A person or business that people work for. page 16

employment agency A group of people who work to find jobs for others. page 17

Equal Employment Opportunity Commission (EEOC) A federal agency that makes sure that laws against job discrimination are obeyed. page 111

experience The past practice and training you have from doing a job before. page 20

F

family practitioner A doctor who is trained to treat both children and adults. page 89

fare The money you pay to ride in a bus, train, plane, or taxi. page 54

federal income tax The tax money you pay to the United States government on money you earn. page 80

fees The money people pay when they receive services. page 17

firmly Strongly. page 43

G

gossip To talk about people when they are not there. page 72

gross salary The full amount of money you earn during a pay period. page 78

H

health insurance Insurance that helps you pay for different types of health care. page 88

Health Maintenance Organization (HMO) A group of doctors and hospitals that have agreed to provide medical services at a special rate to their members. page 91

hire To give a person a job and pay them for their work. page 31

HIV infection The virus that causes AIDS. page 101

hospitalization insurance Insurance that pays part of the cost of staying in a hospital. page 90

I

illegal Against the law. page 107

illegal aliens People who come to the United States from other nations without the permission of the United States government. page 110

impression How you make another person think and feel about you. page 26

independent Being able to work by yourself without asking for help all the time. page 71

Internal Revenue Service (IRS) The government agency that collects federal income taxes. page 82

internist A doctor who treats diseases and problems found in adults. page 89

J

job counselor A person at an employment agency who helps you find a job. page 17

job interview A meeting between an employer and a person who wants a job. page 17

K

kidney failure A sickness in which a person's kidneys stop working. page 99

L

laid off Losing your job because the employer needs fewer workers. page 64

letter of application A letter that you write to an employer to apply for a job. page 28

M

major medical insurance Insurance that pays for very large medical bills, such as surgery. page 90

manual A book that has the company's rules for its workers. It may also have directions for workers about how to use machines and tools. page 62

Medicaid A government health insurance program to provide health care for people with low incomes. page 91

Medicare A government health insurance program that pays for hospital stays for people who are at least 65 years old. page 91

Medicare tax Money used by the government to pay for a health insurance plan for older adults. page 80

minority groups Groups of people in a nation that are not like most people in that nation. For example, the difference may be race or religion. page 108

N

national origin The country where you were born. page 108

net pay The amount of money you can keep from your salary. page 79

P

pediatrician A doctor who treats children. page 89

personality The special way you act and feel. page 7

personnel The people who work for a business or employer. page 20

promotion A better-paying job with more responsibilities for the same company. page 70

R

references People who can give a good report on your work, skills, and personality. page 28

refund Money that is returned to you. page 82

request To ask for something. page 26

responsibilities The jobs and duties of a worker. page 42

resume A summary of information about your education and skills. page 31

retaliation Getting even. page 112

retirement The period when an older person no longer works. page 98

role model A person who sets an example for others to follow. page 6

S

sample An example to show what other things are like. page 42

schedule A plan for getting things done or being at a certain place at a certain time. page 53

severe Very bad or serious. page 101

sexual harassment Acts and words about sex that make you feel uncomfortable on the job. page 108

Social Security A federal program that provides monthly income to many people. page 96

Social Security tax Money used by the government to send a monthly check to older adults. page 80

specialist A doctor who has studied a special area of medicine and has passed special tests. page 89

spouse A husband or wife. page 98

stub The paper attached to a paycheck. It has salary information. page 64

successful Doing something well. page 70

sue To take someone to court. page 110

supervisor The person who is your boss. page 61

Supplemental Security Income (SSI) A Social Security program that pays monthly checks to low-income people who are 65 or disabled. page 98

surgeon A doctor who can operate, or do surgery. page 88

surgery The use of medical tools to operate on the body. page 90

survivors benefits Monthly checks that are paid to certain family members of a worker who has died. page 96

T

talents Your special skills. page 7

tolls The money you pay for the use of some bridges, tunnels, and highways. page 53

transfer A ticket that allows you to ride on a second bus without having to pay a second time. page 54

transportation Different ways to travel, such as by cars, trains, and buses. page 52

U

unemployment insurance Insurance for workers who lose their jobs. page 64

V

values Ideas, beliefs, and actions that are important to you. page 8

volunteer Doing a job without getting paid. page 9

W

workers' compensation Insurance that pays medical bills of people who get hurt while working. It may pay part of the salary to a worker who gets hurt and cannot work. page 64

INDEX

ANSWER KEY

Chapter 1
Page 12 Workshop
Answers will vary: 1, 2, or 3.

Page 13 Workshop Practice
1. You need to like physical work and being with animals.
2. Any four of the following are correct: electrician, carpenter, bricklayer, painter, plumber, and roofer.
3. You need to be friendly and enjoy talking to other people. You also need to be a good listener.
4. Any four of the following are correct: nursing aide, dental assistant, ambulance attendant, home care aide, orderly, and physical therapist.
5. You need to like to talk on the telephone and to work indoors at a desk. You need to like typing, word processing, and computer work. You need to know how to keep records and how to file.
6. Any four of the following are correct: police officer, firefighter, letter carrier, garbage collector, cook, waiter, cashier, maintenance worker, and house cleaner.

Pages 13–14 Comprehension
1. True
2. True
3. False; Your personality is important when you choose a job.
4. True
5. False; Improving your skills will help you get a better job.

Page 14 Vocabulary
1. d
2. a
3. e
4. b
5. c

Chapter 2
Page 21 Workshop
1.a. packaging
1.b. $5 per hour
2.a. part-time
2.b. 728-9007
3.a. home improvement
3.b. 5 years

Page 23 Workshop Practice
1. benefits
2. evening
3. full-time
4. required
5. Monday through Friday
6. week
7. experience preferred
8. hour
9. morning
10. afternoon or evening
11. mechanic, mechanical
12. necessary

Pages 23–24 Comprehension
1. They may know of openings at their job. They can ask their employer if there are any job openings where they work. This is the best way to find a job.
2. The job counselor can give you a special test to find out about your talents and skills. You may also take an interest test to find out what kind of work you would enjoy doing. Then the job counselor will help you choose the best kind of work for you.
3. A private employment agency may charge a fee. Private agencies are listed in the Yellow Pages of the telephone book and also in the classified ads.
4. You have to take the civil service test.
5. To find out about job openings, ask your family and friends if there are any openings at their work. You can also look on bulletin boards in schools, supermarkets, and community centers. You can call private and state employment agencies. You can check the classified ads. You can go to personnel offices.

Page 24 Vocabulary

1. employer
2. fee
3. application
4. classified ads
5. personnel
6. experience

Chapter 3
Pages 35–36 Workshop

Answers will vary. Print clearly and fill out the form completely.

Page 38 Workshop Practice

Answers will vary.

Page 38 Vocabulary

1. apply
2. impression
3. references
4. resume
5. hire
6. request

Page 39 Comprehension

People often apply for jobs by calling the telephone numbers in the <u>Help Wanted</u> ads. Sometimes people have to go <u>in person</u> to apply for a job. When you go to see the employer, you need to dress <u>neatly</u>. Other times, you may have to write a letter of <u>application</u> that tells why you would be good for the job. It is against the law for an employer to refuse to hire you because of your age, sex, <u>race</u>, or <u>religion</u>.

Chapter 4
Page 48 Workshop

Answers will vary. Keep your answers brief and exact.

Page 49 Workshop Practice

Any six are correct. Answers can be in any order.

1. Find out date, time, and place of the interview.
2. Get directions to the place of the interview.
3. Learn about the company.
4. Think about the job skills needed.
5. Have resume, sample application, and social security card.
6. Make list of questions to ask.
7. Practice answering questions.
8. Clean and press clothes.

Page 49 Vocabulary

Answers will vary. You may use more than one vocabulary word in a sentence.

Page 50 Comprehension

1. date, time, and place
2. 10 to 15 minutes early
3. talk about personal problems
4. What responsibilities will I have?
5. the next day

Chapter 5
Page 56 Workshop

1. 8:06 A.M.
2. 7:51 A.M.
3. 15
4. 5:40 P.M.
5. 5:54 P.M.
6. 10:05 A.M.

Page 58 Workshop Practice

Answers will vary.

Pages 58–59 Vocabulary

1. transfer
2. transportation
3. fare
4. toll
5. car-pool

Page 59 Comprehension

1. True
2. False; You need thirty minutes to ride to work and your job starts at 8:00 a.m., so you have to wake up early enough to allow time for eating and getting dressed.
3. True
4. True
5. False; It is more expensive to drive your own car to work than to share expenses in a car-pool.

Chapter 6
Page 67 Workshop

1. All employees must study and obey these safety rules.
2. Workers should report all injuries to the person in charge as soon as possible.
3. Practical jokes are not allowed.
4. Using alcohol or drugs is not allowed. Employees taking prescribed drugs that may affect their work need to report this fact to their supervisors.
5. Employees are not allowed to hang clothing on walls or behind doors.
6. Employees are not allowed to smoke in storerooms, battery rooms, or in other areas where dangerous materials are kept.
7. Workers are not allowed to wear loose chains, key chains, or unnecessary metal when working near electricity.

Page 68 Workshop Practice

1. Rule 11
2. Rule 5
3. Rule 4
4. Rule 7
5. Rule 3
6. Rule 13
7. Rule 9
8. Rule 9

Page 68 Vocabulary

1. laid off
2. benefit
3. alcohol
4. supervisors
5. manual
6. co-workers

Page 69 Comprehension

1. stealing supplies
2. factory work
3. They help cause accidents.
4. unemployment insurance
5. workers' compensation

Chapter 7
Page 75 Workshop

1. Lauren needs to accept criticism and to learn from her mistakes. She needs to stop talking to her co-workers and work faster. She needs to work more carefully so she will not leave paper on the floor.
2. Lauren should not ask co-workers to do her work. She could ask her supervisor to explain the directions again.

Page 76 Workshop Practice
Check marks by 1, 2, 4, and 6.

Page 76 Vocabulary

1. c
2. e
3. f
4. a
5. b
6. d

Page 77 Comprehension
Being a dependable and <u>cooperative</u> worker will help you succeed at work. Having the right attitude can also help you <u>succeed</u> at

your job. Learn to accept <u>criticism</u> from supervisors. When you do something wrong, be willing to learn from your <u>mistakes</u>. Your supervisor wants you to obey all <u>safety</u> rules. To get along with other workers, sometimes you may have to give in a little and <u>compromise</u>. If you are a good worker, you may earn a <u>raise</u> in salary. If you get job training, you may even get a <u>promotion</u> to a better job.

Chapter 8
Page 84 Workshop
1. 2
2. yes
3. no
4. 111-22-3333
5. 4

Page 86 Workshop Practice
Answers will vary. You may have some blanks, just as Adam did.

Page 87 Vocabulary
Answers will vary. You may use more than one vocabulary word in a sentence.

Page 87 Comprehension
1.a. $346.15 **1.b.** $1,500
2. Gross salary is the full amount of money you earn before any deductions. Net pay is the money you take home after deductions.
3. FICA money is used to pay older adults a monthly income. Medicare taxes pay for health insurance for older adults.
4. Many workers have a deduction for taxes or health insurance.

5. A job may offer paid sick days. Other benefits may include paid vacation, a group health insurance plan, and a retirement plan.

Chapter 9
Page 92 Workshop
1. Jesse C. Rivera, her son
2. Central Animal Hospital
3. He slipped on a wet floor and turned his ankle.
4. All American Insurance

Page 94 Workshop Practice
The answers on the form will vary. Print clearly and fill out the form completely.

Pages 94–95 Comprehension
1. Friends can tell you about doctors they like. You can call a nearby hospital or your insurance company and ask them to suggest a doctor.
2. People need hospitalization, medical, and major medical insurance.
3. Many people buy group health insurance because group plans cost less than private plans and may be provided through the company where the people work.
4. Many people join an HMO to pay less for health care. Members pay a fee to join the HMO and get a special rate for medical care—doctor visits, surgery, and hospital stays.

5. Medicare is a government health insurance program for people 65 and older. Medicaid is another government health insurance program for people with low incomes.

Page 95 Vocabulary
1. family practitioner
2. specialist
3. Hospitalization
4. Major medical
5. surgeon

Chapter 10
Pages 102–103 Workshop
1. no
2. Lauren Jessica Johnson
3. no
4. Donna Mary Mason
5. Henry Paul Johnson
6. Lauren Jessica Brown

Page 104 Workshop Practice
The answers on the form will vary. Print clearly and fill out the form completely. Do not use any abbreviations on the form.

Page 105 Vocabulary
Answers will vary. You may use more than one vocabulary word in a sentence.

Page 105 Comprehension
1. The government gets money to pay Social Security benefits from Social Security taxes that workers pay.
2. A person needs to earn 40 credits in order to receive the most Social Security benefits.

3. Workers who become disabled, a deceased worker's spouse who is disabled, children with disabilities who are over age 18, and people who cannot work because they have AIDS or HIV infection can get Social Security disability benefits.
4. The spouse who takes care of the deceased worker's children, the deceased worker's children, a deceased worker's child who is disabled, and a spouse age 60 and over can get survivors benefits.
5. People with low incomes who are blind, disabled, or over age 65, or who have children with disabilities, can get Supplemental Security Income.

Chapter 11
Pages 112–113 Workshop
1. Smith's Box Company
2. typing
3. 65 words a minute
4. 50 words a minute
5. She feels she was not hired because she is deaf.

Page 114 Workshop Practice
Check "sex" as the cause of discrimination. Answers will vary. Include the idea that Janet feels she was fired because she is a woman and not because she is a slow or a poor worker.

Page 115 Vocabulary

Answers will vary. You may use more than one vocabulary word in a sentence.

Page 115 Comprehension

People may face discrimination because of their age, race, sex, religion, <u>disability</u>, or <u>national origin</u>. People may face <u>job</u> discrimination from employers. An employer cannot refuse to hire a <u>pregnant</u> woman. People may face <u>housing</u> discrimination when they want to buy or rent a home. The first important law to end discrimination was the <u>Civil Rights Act</u> of 1964.